DOG PARK

A NOVEL

MICHELLE O'NEIL

Publishing Services provided by Paper Raven Books LLC
Printed in the United States of America
First Printing, 2024

ISBN 979-8-9914143-0-2 (paperback)

This is a work of fiction. Names, characters, businesses, events and incidents are the products of the author's imagination. Any resemblance to actual persons, living or dead, or actual events is purely coincidental, except for Choco, who was quite real.

For Todd, Riley, Seth, and Yip

CHAPTER 1

Shooting Lessons

The day Becky turned eight, she found herself in a cornfield wearing a pink twirly skirt, holding her father Bruce's handgun. Their two Siberian huskies ran circles around her, then took off to explore. Becky loved her dogs, and she loved that skirt, a gift from her mother, Katie. Pink was her favorite color. The skirt had two layers of tulle, which gave it lift and a little bounce. Wearing it, she felt like a ballerina. Becky meant to leave it at her mother's. In all the excitement of her birthday celebration, she'd forgotten to change clothes before returning to Bruce.

Becky knelt on the floor greeting their dogs and noticed Bruce rolling his eyes at the sight of her new skirt. Beretta and Magnum sniffed Becky from head to toe whenever she returned from Katie's.

Bruce told Becky they were going somewhere special. She was full of cake and ice cream and happy birthday wishes, and full of longing for her mother, whom she only got to see every other weekend. Becky felt like playing with her new Barbies in her bedroom but was curious about what her father had planned. Bruce smiled at her and patted his leg twice for the huskies to come. Outside, he helped the dogs up into the bed of his pickup truck.

They drove off the highway and onto a dirt road and from there into a cornfield.

"What's out here, Daddy?" Becky asked, covering her eyes with her hand against the late afternoon sun.

"This is our gun range, Becky. It's time you learned to shoot."

Becky's dark brown eyes widened. "Daddy, kids aren't allowed to shoot guns."

Bruce replied, "*Little* kids aren't allowed to handle guns, and *dumb* kids aren't allowed to handle guns, but you are neither of those things, Becky. You have a Second Amendment right to protect yourself, and it's important you know how to use it. There are a lot of psychos out there who would love to hurt a little girl like you."

Becky bit her lip. Her eyes darted side to side as she considered what her mommy would say, wishing she could just go back to Katie's house. Back to cake and blowing out candles. Back to Barbie dolls and roller skates. Back to Katie braiding Becky's long dark hair. Katie hated guns and hated knowing Bruce kept one at his house. When they'd been married, it made Katie nervous, especially with his temper. They had divorced before Becky made it to toddlerhood, and since that time, Katie had repeatedly asked Bruce to get a safe for it.

Becky heard him say on numerous occasions, "Katie, I am not an imbecile," or sometimes, "Katie, don't try to act like you know shit about guns."

Bruce refused to lock up the gun. How would he be able to access it quickly if it were locked in a safe? He told Becky to never touch it and trusted she wouldn't.

When a school shooter killed a bunch of first graders in a state far away, Katie and her new husband Evan brought Becky and her baby brothers Joey and Jack on a march for common-sense gun laws. Bruce was always correcting Becky to refer to them as her *half-brothers*, but Katie said that wasn't necessary. There were many tearful speeches at the vigil. Becky liked how she got to hold a battery-operated candle. It felt like she was in a sky of twinkling stars, thousands of lights shining in the dark for those kids. There were pictures of the child victims everywhere. All the grown-ups were sad and determined this would never happen again, but it *had* happened since in other schools in other states. Becky hated the drills at school where they had to turn off the lights and hide in the closet in case a shooter was on the loose. Having to pretend no one was in the room so he'd go shoot up another class instead of hers made Becky feel guilty in addition to being afraid.

Becky remembered Bruce slamming his hand down on the supper table after finding out Katie took her to the vigil. He called them, "A bunch of idiots who do not realize if the school had armed protection, that little fucker never would have gotten in to shoot up those kids in the first place."

After Bruce stopped the truck, he lowered the tailgate, and the huskies leapt out of the back. Pulling his handgun out from under the driver's seat, he tucked it into his waistband and knelt to face Becky. Hands firmly on her shoulders, he looked into her big brown eyes, which incidentally looked just like his. "Becky, guns are not the problem. Bad people are the problem. The only thing to protect us from bad guys is having guns of our own. That's just how it is. *That's* how we win." Letting go of her shoulders, Bruce stood up.

Becky's insides twisted, and her head began to ache. She put the palms of both hands on her forehead, closed her eyes, and pressed. She was forever caught between her parents.

Bruce led Becky to a secluded section on a long hollow row between two tall rows of corn. There was a target set up at the end of it. He showed her how to roll out a big piece of paper with the shape of a man on it and tack it up on the target.

Becky had always known about the gun. She knew Bruce kept it hidden in the drawer of his bedside table, under his naked-lady magazines. There wasn't an inch of their little house Becky hadn't explored. She knew about the condoms in the back of his underwear drawer, if not exactly what they were for. She knew about the picture of him and her mother he'd scratched Katie's face out of. Bruce kept it in a shoebox with his wrestling ribbons and trophies under his bed. Katie had been wearing her cheerleader outfit and Bruce his football uniform in the photo. He was smiling, and Katie had probably been smiling too. Becky wondered what it would have looked like for her parents to be together and happy.

Bruce pointed at the target.

"Me and my buddies from Malone's use it all the time. I come out here when you're with your mother."

Demonstrating how to hold the gun, Bruce said, "Never point it at anyone you don't intend to kill." He added, "You not only gotta know your target—you also gotta know what's *behind* your target." This seemed like very important and grown-up information, and despite feeling she might get in trouble with Katie, she was proud he was trusting her this way. Becky grinned up at her daddy. The truth was she was equally smitten with each parent and looked at both with starry eyes.

"That bullet will go right through your target and into someone else in the next room if you aren't careful," he said.

Becky nodded, imagining a bullet traveling through someone and then through someone else in the next room in a cartoonish way. BAM! They hopped right back up, a hole in their body. At eight years old, Becky could not imagine ever shooting anyone for real. She couldn't imagine real blood or real death. The gun felt heavy in her hands. Bruce stood behind and wrapped his arms around her. He clamped his large hands around hers.

"Now, remember. Everyone is scared when they take their first shot. It don't matter if you're scared—you gotta do it anyway, Becks. You are a tough girl. You are *not* a pussy. Now use your finger to pull the trigger! Just shoot. Don't worry about hitting nothin' this first time."

Becky closed her eyes and pulled the trigger. The gun held steady because he was holding it steady, but it stung her hands. She shuddered. His body felt smothering wrapped around her. She wanted to squirm out of his grip and run.

"Pull the trigger again, Becky," he commanded. "Do it!"

Becky closed her eyes and pulled the trigger. POP!

After two more shots, Bruce took his hands off hers and watched from the side.

Becky squinted her eyes, aiming the gun straight ahead. Her arms began to shake.

"C'mon, Becky. Strong arms. Jesus Christ."

She straightened her arms, squeezed her eyes shut, and pulled the trigger again. POP! The gun kicked up toward the sky.

"Goddammit, Becky. You can't close your eyes."

Becky opened her eyes, tilted her head to the side. POP!

Her right hand held the gun, and she let it drop down by her side. She pulled her left arm back toward her chest, shaking it as if she'd touched something gross or slimy.

"Hey! You're still holding a real gun in your hand."

"I know," Becky said.

"Well, then get your damn finger off the trigger when you ain't shooting."

A pause.

"Okay, now, do it again, Becky."

POP! POP!

Bullet casings flew back and hit her in the head.

"Ow!" Becky cried.

"It won't hurt ya. Keep going. You just gotta ignore it."

POP! POP! POP!

"Good job, Becky. That's my girl!"

POP!

"Aim lower, Becks. Look through the sight. Look through the *sight*."

She squinted her eyes and turned to look at him, confused.

He took the gun from her. "The sight is right in the center. Look here. Not above it. Not below it."

He handed back the gun.

There were too many instructions. Her hands hurt. The noise hurt her ears. Tears streamed down Becky's face. With each pull of the trigger, her pink twirly skirt bounced and shook.

Becky thought of what her mother would say, and it made her head hurt more.

Imagining the kids in her class cowering and crying and hurting, was Becky *with* those kids? Or was she the shooter? Or was she the good guy with the gun that could save them?

Finally, they were out of bullets.

Bruce nodded. "You did good, Becks. I just want to run through the safety rules one more time while we're out in the field."

Bruce stood, solemn as a Boy Scout reciting the Pledge of Allegiance.

"Repeat after me. Always keep the gun pointed in a safe direction."

"Always keep the gun pointed in a safe direction," Becky repeated, her voice quivering.

"Always keep your finger *off the trigger* until you are ready to shoot."

"Always keep your finger off the trigger until you are ready to shoot," Becky said.

"Always know where you're aiming."

"Always know where you're aiming," Becky repeated.

"And there's just one more rule you need to promise to obey. Do you promise?"

She nodded. "I promise."

"You cannot tell your mother or anyone else you're learning to shoot. They'd make a big deal of it because they think you're a baby, but you're not. You're eight now, and you deserve to know how to protect yourself."

Becky tried to smile; she knew it was what he wanted. A lump formed in her throat.

"I'm proud of you, Becks. And remember, you promised not to tell, and you can't break a promise."

She nodded.

"That's my girl," Bruce said.

He whistled for Beretta and Magnum, and they came running from deep within the cornfield. When they got home, Becky went into her bedroom and changed out of her skirt. She tucked it in the back of her closet where it would stay until she saw her mother again.

Becky never told her mother about the shooting lessons. By the time she was 13, she had given up pink entirely and wore only dark grungy clothes. She hardly brushed her thick dark hair. Rail thin, she walked with shoulders slumped forward, head down. She wore thick dark eyeliner and black high-top sneakers.

Becky no longer looked at her father with starry eyes, and her mother, Katie, was dead.

By the time Becky was 14, they had a third dog, and she'd become a better shot than Bruce. His response was to stop taking her to the gun range entirely.

CHAPTER 2

A Chewed-Up Sofa

Becky stayed after school to help her art teacher set up a student exhibit. The sky was turning to dusk as Mr. Damon pulled up to her house to drop her off. They both noticed the couch on the curb, its white stuffing spilling out of it.

"*Fuck*," Becky thought. It was the one piece of furniture they had that wasn't a total embarrassment. Their elderly neighbor recently gave it to them when he moved into a retirement community. Noting Bruce's truck in the driveway, Becky hopped out of the car quickly, thanking Mr. Damon for the ride. She had to get to the dogs.

Inside, the two older huskies huddled in the corner of the living room. They were each curled tightly into a ball, tails between their legs. The new dog, the younger one, was nowhere to be seen.

"Where's Ruger?" Becky asked, eyes darting all over the room.

Bruce sat at the kitchen table, a can of beer in one hand, his handgun in the other. Taking a swig of beer and staring straight ahead, he said, "He's out back, and he's lucky I didn't shoot him."

Becky rushed out onto the back porch, and there was Ruger, eight months old. She ran her hand over his body, causing him to flinch. Becky could only imagine what Bruce had done to him. Panting heavily, Ruger lifted his head and then laid it down on the floor again.

Becky sat on the cold porch floor next to Ruger. Wrapping her arms around her knees, she began to sob. She wished she could talk to her mom. She missed her so much. Even though Katie had abandoned her by giving up custody when she was seven, she'd always been open to hearing Becky's complaints about Bruce. For years, every other weekend, Katie left her new husband and their two little boys in Charleston and made the four-hour drive to see her. That ended seven months ago when Katie passed tragically.

After Bruce went to sleep, Becky snuck Ruger back into the house where he slept on a towel on the floor at the foot of her bed.

The next week, Becky's art teacher, Mr. Damon, asked about the situation with the dog that ate their couch. Becky responded as if it were a funny thing that happened. She kept it light, even though it devastated her that Bruce had beaten Ruger.

"How old is he? How much exercise does he get?" Mr. Damon asked.

"He's, like, eight months old. He plays with our other two dogs in the yard sometimes."

"Oh, Becky, he's a puppy! He's going to need a lot more exercise than that," Mr. Damon said, putting his hand on his hip and cocking his head to the side, looking at her painting in progress. "Siberian huskies can get very destructive if they're cooped up. But get them out, let them run? They are *good* dogs. Think about it. They were bred to pull sleds across the snow for hundreds of miles. He's going nuts with boredom. He's going stir crazy! He needs a job! Get him somewhere he can run, and he'll be a different boy. Take that dog to a dog park." Mr. Damon winked at her, before walking away to check the next student's work.

Becky stepped back to look at her painting. When she drew or painted, it was almost as if she went to a different world. She couldn't remember putting red here, or blue there, or the little touch of yellow in the corner. But somehow, she liked the outcome. Art class was one of the only times she felt calm and relaxed. Mr. Damon was often encouraging Becky to consider going to college for art after graduating high school. He acted like it was a given. Katie had always encouraged Becky's creative spirit as well. Becky had three more years of high school to worry about before that. For now, she just needed to figure out how to convince Bruce to take the huskies to the dog park.

CHAPTER 3

The Damned Dog Park

When Bruce was in tenth grade, his father moved the family from their home in rural Pennsylvania, to South Carolina because he'd taken a factory job at the Pepsi plant in Haberland City. Bruce had not been popular in school previously, but his athleticism, his quiet brooding, and his "new kid" status gave him a certain mystery Becky's mother Katie had responded to.

As a boy, Bruce always wanted a dog, but his father would not allow it. Bruce had never been sure whether his father didn't like dogs or just didn't want to see Bruce happy.

"You bring home a puppy, and I'll shoot it," he'd threatened 10-year-old Bruce when he mentioned the neighbor's husky mix recently had pups.

Bruce liked huskies because they reminded him of wolves. His mother, a small, meek woman, knew this and found curtains with wolves on them at a discount store. She used thumbtacks to hang them in her son's bedroom, her small acts of kindness, a penance for not protecting him from his father's wrath, both physical and emotional. Bruce's first memory was of his dad pushing him down when he was four years old, encouraging Bruce to get up and fight him, and then pushing him down again. Sometimes he could still picture his father's face, teasing and menacing, "Get up, shit-for-brains! Hit me back. Don't be a pussy." If Bruce were to cry, he'd get "something to cry about" by way of a spanking. He walked on eggshells his entire childhood, fearing the man.

To Bruce, wolves were majestic. They seemed wild and strong and unafraid.

Bruce always thought of wolves as his spirit animal and in an unguarded moment recently said so to Becky. She'd rolled her eyes and told him he couldn't say that because he wasn't Native American; it was *"cultural appropriation,"* or some bullshit. He wondered where that kid got all her ideas. She'd gotten increasingly mouthy with him as of late.

Becky was 14 now, and he could feel her slipping away. She hadn't hugged his neck in probably two years and every day was looking more and more like a woman. While she didn't have her mother's blond hair, and looked more like his side, she was starting to resemble Katie in certain other ways. It made him avert his eyes, and they both felt the distance and didn't know what to do with it.

The school strongly suggested Becky see a counselor after her mother died, but after two sessions, she didn't want to go, and Bruce wasn't about to force it. Some shrink prying into their family business? No, thank you.

But lately, it seemed Becky truly hated him. *Teenagers,* he thought. It wasn't as if *he* had anything to do with Katie's death. Katie had done that all on her own, not paying attention behind the wheel. It wasn't fair to make him pay the price for it.

Bruce had gotten Beretta, their first husky, when Becky was a baby, right after Katie had left him. They were splitting custody at the time. He'd gotten Magnum, the second husky, when Katie gave up parental rights and he got full custody. He thought a puppy might cheer his daughter up after Katie moved to Charleston with her new family, and it did, some. Now they had a third husky, the pup, Ruger. That, also an attempt to cheer Becky after Katie died, but it hadn't worked.

The first two dogs had been no trouble, but Bruce wondered if Ruger didn't have a screw loose. He'd been harder to house train, lifting his leg wherever he pleased. He didn't listen. He chewed up shoes, table legs, and, once, Bruce's favorite leather belt. And then, of course there was the sofa he'd ruined. It had been a few weeks, and it still chapped Bruce's ass to be sitting on an uncomfortable half-broken recliner when he watched TV.

After dinner one night, Becky got up her nerve and broached the dog park subject with her father. Bruce's first reaction was, "I didn't ask for and am not taking advice from that fairy art teacher. He wears *nail polish*, Becky. What does he know about dogs?"

"Mr. Damon has a lot of experience with dogs, Dad. His parents used to breed them. He says maybe taking Ruger for a run would help, or to a dog park where he can exercise. Or agility training. He says it might get some of his destructive energy out. Dogs like Ruger, *like wolves*, can't be cooped up all the time."

"The other dogs never mind being cooped up."

"Well, Ruger is different. We have to respect his temperament."

Becky the know-it-all, he thought. *And now I'm supposed to "respect" a dog?*

Becky continued, "And the other dogs probably do mind it. They are probably bored and depressed too. They just don't get destructive like he does."

Bruce was sick to death of hearing Becky talk about Mr. Damon. It was Mr. Damon this, and Mr. Damon that. At open house night, he'd been glad to see Mr. Damon was *a faggot*. At least he wouldn't be making any passes at his teenage daughter. She obviously *loved* him, the value she placed on his every word, when she did nothing but roll her eyes at her own father.

"I have not gone running since my football days, Becks, and I don't have time to go to a damned dog park."

"Dad, you do. It's just five miles away, and they'd only need to be there for a half-hour to get their energy out. What else are you going to do besides sit in front of the TV and drink beer?"

"Becky, that's enough lip outta you. Go do those dishes. Now."

She stomped into the kitchen and began vigorously scrubbing the plates, clanking the pots and pans loudly. After finishing, she escaped into her bedroom.

Becky kept her room dark. A blue lightbulb on her side table was often all she used for light. Lying on her bed, the dim room somehow helped calm her nerves. Back when her parents were together, before she could even remember, her mother had made a whole girly room for her, but Becky painted white over the pink walls a few months ago. She wasn't a little girl anymore, and pink was too happy a color. She was sick of it. There was a David Bowie poster, and a Salvador Dalí print of a clock that appeared to be melting and dripping down a shelf. She bought it in the gift store on a field trip to a museum with her art class. Other than that, her walls were covered with her own drawings.

Sketch after sketch of a gaunt, dark-haired teen girl with a long nose, cheeks sunken in, collarbones poking out. The girl curled in on herself, folded up as if actively protecting her internal organs, her heart, from a beating. In most of the sketches, messy hair covered the girl's eyes. In the ones that did show her eyes, there was a sadness so deep and pleading it was unnerving for others to look at.

More than once, Becky overheard other students in the school art room comment, "Creepy."

"You just keep sketching, Becky. Keep painting," Mr. Damon told her. "Get it all out."

"You really think I could get into art school one day?" she asked him, biting her lip.

He replied, "Becky, you *absolutely* have what it takes to get into the best art colleges in the country."

Anyone paying attention could have seen these were self-portraits, but Bruce took little interest in Becky's artwork and rarely if ever went into her bedroom. The few times Becky brought up art school, Bruce said, "No money in art, Becky." Or, "College ain't worth it these days."

Bruce stewed about the dog park in uneasy silence for a week. Then Ruger chewed up one of his work boots.

Becky had been home when it was discovered and threw herself in front of the puppy to protect him.

"It's not his fault, Dad!" she screamed. "I told you—he's not the kind of dog that can be cooped up inside all day!"

The next night after supper, when Becky was doing the dishes, Bruce said, "Finish up, then help me get the dogs in the truck. I guess we'll give that damned dog park a try."

Becky quickly finished scrubbing the skillet in the sink.

The two older dogs needed a boost to get up into the back of Bruce's truck. Becky brought Ruger into the front cab, fearing he'd leap out of the bed on the way over if they let him ride in back. Wrapping her arms around him, she hoped Lake Woof would be the answer as they drove up a hill toward the park.

Pulling into the parking lot, the dogs were wild with curiosity and excitement. They stretched their noses into the air, sniffing hard. Becky hooked Ruger's leash to his collar and opened the door of the truck. The two older dogs walked off-leash next to Bruce. Ruger was strong and hard to control, and Bruce chastised Becky. With a look of pure hatred on her face, she gave him the finger behind his back on their way into the large dog section.

Bruce saw a brown-and-white pit bull, and a sleek black Labrador retriever mix across the park, frolicking and playing. He nodded for Becky to unhook Ruger's leash from his collar, and soon, all three huskies were running free, all the way across the park. It was a beautiful thing to see, like watching wild horses gallop across a prairie. Becky looked at Bruce and smiled. A rare moment of connection. The dogs ran for 45 minutes that day, back and forth from one side of the park, to the other. They stopped to sniff every inch of it. They peed on every pole, every garbage can, every tree. The park wasn't crowded. Only a few other dogs were there, coming and going, and their dogs pretty much stayed to themselves, running in their own little pack.

When they got home, Bruce and Becky were both in a good mood. She made them nachos for a snack and joined him for a whole episode of *Pawn Stars*, which Becky rarely did anymore.

The dogs slept all evening and all night. The puppy got into no trouble the next day. Or the day after that. Bruce thought, *Well, I'll be damned. Maybe that art teacher was right after all. Ruger just needs to get his energy out. Alrighty then.*

They got into a routine of taking all three dogs every Saturday and a couple of times during the week when his schedule would allow. Bruce worked a rotating shift at the warehouse, so sometimes it was mornings; sometimes it was evenings. It seemed to be doing the trick. Ruger hadn't destroyed anything since they started coming to Lake Woof. Bruce was nodding politely at the other dog owners, doing his best to be social. He even picked up his dogs' poop sometimes, which was disgusting, but part of the rules. He knew he'd look like a real asshole if he made Becky do it every time.

People congregated in a gazebo in the center of the park, and he meandered over where the conversation was happening. He'd never been good around people unless he had a few drinks in him, but found the fresh air put him in a decent mood. The dogs were good. Becky was being nicer to him. Maybe life wasn't all that bad.

A woman who appeared to be in her 60s and wearing a Yankees cap nodded and smiled at him, welcoming them into the conversation. "Beautiful dogs," she said in a thick Bronx accent.

"Thank you, ma'am," he said in response. "They're Siberian huskies."

Smiling at him, she said, "They look like they're part wolf!"

Bruce beamed.

"They have a lot of energy," she added.

"That they do."

"My name is Nancy, and this is Teddy," she said. "He's the opposite, 100 percent lazy," she laughed, and Bruce laughed with her.

"I'm Bruce," he said, sticking out his hand to shake hers. Nodding toward Becky, he said, "This is my daughter, Becky."

Becky had been looking at the ground. She lifted her eyes to peer through her dark bangs, offering Nancy an embarrassed half smile, and rolled her eyes.

CHAPTER 4

Ann and Choco

Ann's therapist suggested a dog park.

"A dog park?" Ann responded sharply, pulling her blue pashmina wrap around her shoulders tighter. Shifting in her seat, she crossed her arms over her chest, looked him in the eye, and said, "*That's* going to fix everything?"

Ann had not taught a class at the university in months. After the funeral, after the casseroles and the phone calls from well-meaning friends and colleagues, after a mountain of details, came an excruciating quiet. She had not been out of the house and had talked to almost no one. Ann almost always had perfect manners, but now let the phone go to voicemail and stopped responding to texts, even from her best friend Helen, whom she'd known since first grade. Helen was an attorney. Ann, a college professor. Both would be 50 the following year.

Ann had never married, and Helen found herself single several years ago after a contentious divorce. They normally met for dinner once a week to discuss every little detail of their lives. They normally went to concerts and a monthly book group, and to literary events happening downtown or at the college. They normally talked on the phone at least every other day and often made road trips to visit art museums and concerts on the weekends. But normal had been turned upside down. Ann couldn't find the strength to pick up the phone, even for Helen.

Ann had always been put together. Everyone said so. She loved fashion and prided herself on being able to look casual yet sophisticated. She'd taken ballet throughout her childhood, and as an adult her posture was usually practically perfect. Now, she found herself slumping through her days in old t-shirts and sweats. The golden highlights in her shoulder-length brown hair had grown out, making dark roots prominent for several inches at her crown. She'd practiced yoga and Pilates for the last 20 years and was quite fit at 49 years old, but her body ached from lack of movement. She'd been raised Christian but in her 30s had leaned away from religion. She started a Buddhist meditation practice 15 years ago, but that didn't seem to be helping her now. No amount of exercise, meditation, or "positive vibes" would ever be able to take away the unbearable feelings of despair that came with losing her only child. Ann no longer could access any amount of joy in life and longed for an escape from the pain.

She was not on any prescription drugs she could use to overdose. Ann had no gun and would never shoot herself. What a traumatic mess that would be for someone to clean up. Hanging didn't suit her. Ann didn't think she'd have the nerve to kick the stool out from under. She wouldn't know how to tie a proper noose, for that matter. Driving off a cliff was always an option, but again, the poor EMT would have to pull her body from the wreckage. She couldn't bear doing that to anyone. She fantasized about a lethal injection. It would be perfect. If only she could lie down on a blanket in a sunny meadow, neat and tidy. She would look up at a clear blue sky and feel the relief of her pain, the way they humanely put down animals when they were suffering.

Ann hadn't told her therapist she was having suicidal daydreams, but he met her eyes and smiled softly. "Ann, nothing is ever going to *fix* your great loss. But you've got to decide if you want to live or not, and you do have your son's dog to take care of."

Ann tipped her head to the side, impressed he'd seen through her. She swallowed hard and nodded.

Ann agreed to take Choco to the dog park for 30 minutes, and if it went well, another 30-minute visit later in the week. If it was too much, she could quickly leave, and no one would care. It wasn't as big a commitment as lunch with a friend or signing up for a support group which she had no interest in attending. Somehow her loss didn't seem the same as someone who lost a parent who had lived a long life, or even the loss for a parent who had more than one child. She didn't want Liam added to a collective mix. The therapist assured Ann if the dog park didn't feel right, she never had to go back. He said fresh air and light socialization would be good for her, and there was no denying the healing power of dogs. He had two rescues of his own.

Choco wagged his tail and circled Ann's legs as she got his leash from a cubby in the bench/shoe rack/coat rack she and Liam had assembled three years ago. The thing was nearly impossible to put together, and Liam had cussed in frustration. It was the first time he'd used profanity openly in front of her, and she'd said nothing to reprimand him. The unit looked nice in the hall entry of their big historic Victorian home, though Liam's shoes had continued to land in a heap on the floor in front of it rather than tucked neatly into the cubbies as Ann had envisioned.

Choco reached out with his stubby front legs and lifted his hindquarters into the air, making his Dachshund body impossibly longer. Other than pouring him bowls of food and letting him out three times a day, she'd been neglecting him. Guilt gripped Ann's solar plexus. After all, none of this was Choco's fault.

In the new Volvo that Ann hated, Choco stood on his tippy toes in the passenger's seat. His front paws rested on the open window frame, his nose high in the air and his long ears flapping in the wind. Choco had learned how to open automatic car windows with his paws years ago, and Liam had been delighted about it. They knew he was too short to leap out, so they allowed him to do it because it was cute.

Riding through town the smells of civilization made Choco drunk with joy. His tail wagged furiously.

When Liam went away to college, it took Choco just two nights to win a spot in Ann's bed. She tried to get him to use a doggie bed on the floor, but he was used to sleeping in Liam's bed and made a ridiculous fuss. Crying and whining, his large black eyes pleaded with her. He slammed into her bed repeatedly, attempting to leap up onto it. Ann finally picked him up and let him under the covers. It turned out it was nice having Choco there to keep her warm, a living hot water bottle pressed up against her. Ann ended up getting some doggie stairs for her bed.

Back when Liam was eight years old, Ann never thought about the fact he would go off to college one day and she'd be stuck with his dog. It seemed so far away at the time. Dachshunds, she would learn, had a life expectancy of 14, and there were reports of them living up to 18 years. If Choco were among the lucky, she'd hoped

Liam would take him after he finished college. It would have meant a lot to her son, who thought of Choco as the sibling he'd never had. Over the years, Choco had earned many nicknames, but the one most used by Liam was "Bruh." Brother.

Ann turned the Volvo into the greater park and followed a long winding road. Wooden corral-type fencing lined each side. A paved trail ran along one side of the road, and people were walking and biking on it. People were out, living. Women pushed babies in strollers. On the other side of the road was an outdoor fitness course, and men with muscles were doing pull-ups and sit-ups and squats.

Further down the road was a lake to the right and a small building for renting kayaks, paddle boats, canoes, and bicycles.

Ann regretted she'd been too busy and self-absorbed to ever take Liam here while he was growing up. He'd been to the park on school field trips, but she'd never taken him herself. They'd never utilized the dog park for Choco.

Ann's fingers gripped the steering wheel tightly, and she drove slowly. The lake disappeared around a bend and then came back into view, and now she could see there were people water-skiing. They were attached not to boats but to an elaborate robotic pulley system, reminding her of the erector sets Liam used to play with. He'd always loved building things. He loved building worlds with Minecraft, and he'd been absolutely obsessed with Lego. Liam finally got too good at putting them together, finishing elaborate (and expensive) structures in just a day or two and immediately yearning for the next set. He wasn't spoiled or bratty about it; he merely set his sights on what he wanted in a wistful, dreamlike way. Somehow Ann would end up buying a new set for him as if drawn by some force he had over her. Perhaps it was the force that came from the dimple in his right cheek, or his mop of blond hair, or maybe it was the force of his dark brown eyes with lashes so long you'd swear the child was wearing mascara. Whatever that force was, it had certainly made Choco manifest. Since he was five years old, Liam had dreamed of having a "hot dog" of his own. He talked incessantly of his future dog and named him Choco. He drew pictures of him. He even slept with a stuffed-animal Dachshund as a placeholder for years before Ann finally caved. Surprising him with that puppy had been the most joyful day of both their lives.

Finally, toward the very back of the park, Ann saw the sign for Lake Woof. She drove up a hill and into the parking lot, hitting the button to close and lock Choco's window. The dog park overlooked the water. Choco hopped around the front seat, his tail wagging frantically. The little Dachshund paced from the window, to Ann, to the window, back to Ann. She tried three times to catch him before grabbing him like a football under her arm and holding him still.

"There," she said, clicking his leash in place.

Ann took a deep breath and, holding Choco on her lap, checked out the scene. Not many people were there. A woman, likely in her 60s, sat on one of the benches in a gazebo in the middle of the green space. A big yellow dog lay on the ground near her feet. An older clean-cut gentleman and a younger man, a few years older than Liam with messy auburn hair, walked together around a paved oval path inside the enclosure. Two mid-sized dogs frolicked ahead of them. One sleek and jet black, the other a squatty brown-and-white pit bull. All of them were going about their day, seemingly happy, oblivious to her sitting in the car, heart ripped out.

Ann's throat tightened, and her hands began to shake. She thought about leaving, but Choco looked up at her with his soulful brown eyes. His body trembled with excitement, and his tail thumped her lap. Ann promised she would give it a try, and she wasn't someone to go back on her word.

Her mind went to Liam, and what he might say. Sometimes when she thought of him, she heard nothing. Like a bell with no ringer. Dead. But sometimes it was as if she could hear him inside her head. The clear voice of a young man: *"You can do this, Mom. Let him have some fun."*

Ann opened the car door.

Walking through the parking lot, her brain felt fuzzy. She couldn't figure out how to open the gate. Lift the lever? Pull it forward, pull it back? Inwardly, she mocked herself. The college professor needed a tutor to open a simple gate. As she fumbled, she felt her throat tighten, tears of frustration just behind her eyes. She was about to turn back toward her car when the lady in the gazebo yelled, in her thick Bronx accent, "Ya gotta pull it up, *then* ya push! Stick your foot underneath the gate to lift it if you need to."

Ann followed her instructions, and the gate opened. She and Choco found themselves in a little holding area. She unhooked his leash and made her way through the second gate with no problem. Choco, tail wagging, ears flapping, ran directly over to the woman in the gazebo and put his paws up onto her lap.

She laughed, scooping him up, letting him lick her face. "Who is this friendly little guy?"

Ann made her way toward them and said, "That's Choco, my son's dog. Sorry, he isn't supposed to jump on people."

"Are you kiddin'? I love this little guy! It's no trouble at all." She scratched behind Choco's ears and sweet-talked him, "Who's a good boy? Who's a little love?"

She gave him scratches all the way down his long spine.

While many Dachshunds were nervous creatures, Choco never had been. He loved everyone and had yet to find a person who didn't love him back. Liam had gone to an alternative "crunchy" K-12 school. After he got Choco, Liam became anxious about leaving his puppy home alone all day. His teacher, Ms. Julie, was a dog lover herself and invited Choco into the classroom, problem solved. A couple of years later, Choco was officially adopted as the school mascot. They had a ceremony in the school garden for him. Liam read a poem he had written about Choco, and they unveiled a statue of a little Dachshund. Choco pranced through life on stubby legs with the openness of a creature that had never been hurt. He received love and a constant stream of physical handling, serving as unofficial emotional support dog for hundreds of students and faculty alike throughout Liam's school years.

The woman in the gazebo's fat yellow Labrador retriever finally stood up. Choco jumped down off her lap to greet him. Butts were sniffed.

"Thank you for your help with the gate. It's my first time here."

"I didn't think I recognized you. Nice to meet ya. I'm Nancy, and this is Teddy. He's old and arthritic, like me." She laughed, activating a smoker's cough. "He mostly hangs out with me here in the gazebo. Sometimes the big dogs get too *rambunctious* with him. He can't take it, so he stays close," she added.

Ann sat quietly. She watched Choco run all over the enclosure, sniffing.

"The gate is a little warped so it's tricky," Nancy said. "It's like Fort Knox tryin' to get into this place," Nancy laughed.

Teddy tried to hang out with Choco for a few minutes. He lumbered around, lifting his leg to mark a fence post, a tree, then walked out to the furthest part of the green space to make a deposit.

Nancy reached into her fanny pack and took out a poop bag. She limped out across the green space and with obvious effort bent over to pick up Teddy's poop. Slowly, she walked it to a garbage can and dropped it in, then stayed out in the grassy area for a bit, smoking a cigarette.

Ann noticed a couple more dogs making their way into the section. Choco ran over to greet them, and after butt checks, they all began running together. Ann smiled softly watching Choco's joy. He seemed to lift off the ground entirely when he ran.

Nancy made her way back toward Ann, waving her pack of cigarettes in the air. "I had to have my breakfast of champions," she said, before tucking it in her shirt pocket, with a chuckle.

They continued to watch Choco, running around making friends.

"Look at your little hot dog. First day here, and already he's mayor of Lake Woof!" Nancy laughed.

Nancy wasn't the usual person Ann would choose to spend time with, an arthritic smoker with a dog that was morbidly obese. But somehow Nancy was the first person who had not irritated Ann since the accident. Was it because she didn't know and therefore wasn't saying anything useless? Was it because of her kindness with the gate? Was it because she reminded Ann of Penny Marshall from *Laverne and Shirley?* Could it be that her therapist was right, and being out in nature with the sun shining on her face might help her some? It was hard to put a finger on it, but sitting in the gazebo with Nancy, listening to her talk, Ann did feel an almost microscopic shift. She released her first good exhale in months.

They watched Choco march around, wagging his tail, sniffing the sniffs. Alive. Ann turned her head so Nancy couldn't see and blinked her eyes quickly to stave off tears. How was Choco alive and Liam wasn't? It made no sense.

Ann stayed exactly 30 minutes. On the way to her car, she noticed a black pickup truck pull into the parking lot with two Siberian huskies in the back. A stocky dark-haired man got out and nodded at Ann, who offered a faint smile in acknowledgement. A teen girl came around from the passenger's side of the truck with yet another husky.

As Ann got Choco into the car, she watched them make their way across the parking lot. The man walked with a swagger, several feet ahead of the girl. Two of the dogs walked calmly off-leash beside him. The girl, holding tightly to its leash, tried unsuccessfully to control the third dog.

The man, presumably her father, looked back over his shoulder, "Jesus Christ, Becky! Don't let him pull you like that." The daughter glared at him through thick dark bangs that hung long in front of her eyes. And then she gave her father the middle finger behind his back. Ann raised her eyebrows in surprise. She continued to observe as they made their way into the dog park and watched as the three huskies took off in a white blur across the green space. Turning to Choco, who had already curled up in a ball on the front seat, Ann took a breath in. She exhaled, started the car, and began the drive home.

CHAPTER 5

Lake Woof

Lake Woof was divided into two sections, one for small, the other for large dogs. Owners of medium-sized dogs made a choice about which space was better suited for their pups. Choco would officially land in the small-dog section based on weight, but since he was unafraid of big dogs, and since Ann had felt comfortable with Nancy, she decided to go into the big-dog section once again.

On the far end of the dog park, a few tall trees lined the back of the enclosure. In front of the trees was a mountain of dirt. Dogs who loved to dig found great joy there, and dogs who loved to roll in dirt flopped around like pigs at the bottom of the mountain, especially after a rain when there were puddles. There were large concrete industrial pipes in the middle of the green space, put there for play. Some dogs ran through them like tunnels, and some dogs leaped over them entirely as they frolicked and chased. There was a small fenced-in shower on the way out for dogs who got dirty at the park. A community bottle of dog shampoo sat by the hose. People brought it when they thought of it and left it there for the next person.

Sitting in the gazebo with Nancy, Ann noted two gentlemen walking the paved oval path just inside the enclosure, their dogs out ahead of them. She remembered them from her first visit to Lake Woof. Choco ran toward them, yapping hello. The men stopped. The dogs sniffed, checked butts, but then kept walking. Choco followed behind for a while, trying to be part of their group, but eventually, he took a hint and made his way back to Ann and Nancy. Nancy wore a different Yankees t-shirt and sneakers. Ann wore a baggy sweatshirt, an old pair of yoga pants, and slip-on Skechers. She still hadn't done a thing with her hair.

"That's Henry and Rocky," Nancy said, referring to the dogs. "They are BFFs. I'm afraid they only have eyes for each other," she laughed, adding, "Sorry, Choco."

"Are the men father and son?" Ann asked.

"Oh, no, not at all," Nancy said. "They don't have a lick in common, but their dogs, Rocky and Henry, are in *love,* so they've been forced to get to know each other. You should have seen how Ed, the older gentleman, reacted at first," she laughed. "He was, like, get away from me, kid. Tommy is a good kid, but he's *a lot,* if you know what I mean. I'm not a doctor or anything, but I would say he's got ADHD or something. Don't get me wrong—I love him to death, but he just never stops. He takes Rocky for a five-mile run every day and *then* walks laps with Ed. Poor Henry cries at the gate and won't play with the other dogs. He waits at the fence while they run, and when they get back, it's *happy, happy, joy, joy.* Anyway, Tommy seems to idolize Ed."

Ann kept watching the men and their dogs as they walked around the path.

Nancy continued, "Ed's a retired military guy, quiet, all business, straight shooter. Tommy yaps his ear off, but I think they are starting to be honest-to-God friends now. Their dogs met here when Rocky, the pit, was just a puppy, and it was love at first sight." Nancy waved to Ed and Tommy as they rounded the oval. Tommy waved back with his full arm. Even from a distance, Ann could see he had a megawatt smile, all teeth. Ed nodded his head in polite acknowledgement.

An old, rusty van chugged into the parking lot, sounding like it needed a new muffler. A tall muscular man got out of the driver's side and went around to open the back. Ann saw two large dogs standing on a mattress inside. One looked like a Rottweiler, and the other looked like a mastiff. The Rottweiler jumped down and headed toward the fence, and the man bellowed, "STAY!"

Ann noticed tattoos covering his neck, and another tattoo on the side of his face near his temple. His jeans had mud caked on the knees.

The Rottweiler did not obey, and the man stomped after him. Finally catching up with him, he took hold of the dog's leash and yanked hard on the metal choke chain around his neck.

"I said STAY!" he yelled at the dog, who did not crouch or flinch.

Ann grimaced.

Nancy said, "Don't worry about him. He's okay."

"I don't condone being rough with animals," Ann said, shifting her weight on the bench, folding her arms over her chest.

"Oh, I don't condone it either," Nancy said. She shrugged and added, "But I don't worry about them. Those dogs are tanks. He's not really hurting them. And you don't need to worry. Wayne hardly ever brings them inside the park, only lets them run outside the fence. A couple of times when I've convinced him to come in, when it's been just us? His dogs are sweet as can be. And he loves them to death. Wayne isn't a bad guy."

Nancy waved at the man, and he waved back. "Mornin', ma'am." His voice boomed across the park to her.

"How's it going, Wayne?" Nancy yelled back.

Wayne spread his arms wide, looked up at the sky, and said, "Another day in paradise!"

He walked his dogs to the outside of the farthest part of the dog park, and Choco followed, investigating them from inside the fence. Choco barked and play-bowed, and the big dogs returned the gesture. Soon they were running laps along the fence, Choco on the inside, the Rottweiler and mastiff on the outside.

"Damn, that little hot dog can run. He goes full on airborne!" Wayne exclaimed.

Ten minutes later, the big dogs were slowing down, but Choco showed no signs of stopping. Up and down the fence they continued to run.

Nancy smiled and looked down at Teddy. "You gonna run with 'em, Ted? You wanna join 'em?" Teddy lifted his eyes, keeping his chin on the ground.

"No? Okay," she said, shrugging. Then she laughed, which caused her to hack.

Two more dogs entered the park and joined Choco in running the fence with Wayne's dogs.

Ann was starting to feel an affinity for Nancy. It was generous of her to give this man the benefit of the doubt. Ann looked down at her feet and felt shame for judging him so harshly. She knew better. Following in her own father's footsteps, Ann had spent most of her adult life working for social justice. She didn't know what his life was like. Ann just didn't feel like herself anymore.

Later that night in her king-sized bed snuggled up to Choco, Ann was half asleep/half-awake when Liam's face drifted into her mind. His expression beamed love and pride.

"You did good, Mom. Thank you for taking care of him," she imagined Liam saying.

Ann shifted, and Choco sighed. His eyes began darting back and forth under their lids, and his stubby legs began to twitch, reenacting the day's great adventure, running up and down the long fence with the big dogs in his dreams.

CHAPTER 6

Wayne

Becky and Bruce had spent a good hour at the dog park letting their dogs run and were just leaving when Wayne arrived. Passing each other in the parking lot, the younger husky growled at Wayne's dogs which outweighed him by about 60 pounds each. Becky pulled Ruger's leash, trying to control him. The men ignored each other.

Nancy yelled toward the fence, "Wayne! Come on inside. It's just me and Ann here now. Choco won't mind. He loves everyone!"

Wayne waved off her invite and said, "We're good, Nancy. Maybe some other time."

Wayne knew damn well the people at the dog park were afraid of him and his dogs. He knew if he went in there with his big-ass mastiff mix and his Rottie mix, some white lady was going to get scared and cause trouble, and he was not looking for trouble. He was almost two years out after serving a 10-year sentence for a nonviolent cannabis offense in North Carolina. He kept his nose clean. He *minded his own goddamn business.*

Wayne was especially not going to get in any trouble over these damn dogs. However, they each weighed over 100 pounds and needed to get their exercise. If not, they drove him crazy. Thor, the mastiff, he was okay, not too much trouble, but Roach, the Rottie, had always been defiant.

Wayne confided in Nancy more than once, "Roach don't listen. He don't come when I call him. He don't *obey*. He pushes Thor out of the way to get to the food. Roach acts like it don't even affect him when I yank his choke chain."

But as with prisoners, exercise did make Roach act better. A tired Roach was a good Roach. Wayne drove the van over to the dog park. He walked the dogs to the far side of the enclosure and waited for one of them hyper dogs to come in. When they did, he unleashed his two giants and let them run the fence. He knew the other patrons wondered why he bothered coming if he never came in, but he also knew they were relieved he stayed on the outside. He could see it on their faces. Thor and Roach ran up and down the fence with any dog willing to play the game.

The only time he brought them inside the enclosure was when it's empty, or if it's just Nancy.

Her dog didn't run, but she didn't seem scared of Wayne or his dogs. When they got to come inside, Thor and Roach ran all over the grass, sniffing and marking every spot. They loved it. But Wayne never stayed inside long. The chain-link fence looked too much like a prison yard. He preferred being on the outside.

Wayne never met a white lady like Nancy before. She didn't flinch at the tattoos covering his arms or the two on his neck and face. Nancy wasn't afraid Wayne was big and had muscles. She cussed almost as much as he did. Nancy kept it real. She's from New York and talked like it.

Nancy's dog Teddy was big and lazy, and Wayne wished Roach would be lazy too, but he had a long way to go since he was just two years old.

Thor, the mastiff mix, was a joyful dog. Thor could be rough when he was playing, but he meant nothin' by it. Roach was not as friendly. When little kids or even the occasional lady asked, "Can I pet your dog?" Wayne always said, "No, they ain't friendly," but it was really just Roach he'd worried about. Better to stay away from people anyway.

All the dog lovers in the park shared disapproving glances when Wayne yelled at his dogs or when he yanked Roach's leash, but they didn't know what it was like to have a dog this big that wouldn't listen.

One day when it was just him and Nancy, Wayne complained, "He don't obey. That's why I need to rough him up sometimes."

Nancy asked casually, "How old is Roachie?"

Wayne said, "I picked him up about two years ago when I had just got out," stopping to catch himself. Wayne hadn't meant to tell her he'd been in prison.

Nancy didn't flinch. Nodding, she willed him to continue.

"Roach was a small pup then," Wayne continued. "They both were."

Nancy said, "All dogs are different, but maybe think of it like this. What if he isn't trying to defy you, but instead it takes a few minutes for the message to get from his ears to his brain? Maybe he's just not that bright," she chuckled. Wayne laughed too.

"That's for sure," he added.

Later, Wayne got to thinking you couldn't expect a slow kid to know a lot. He had a cousin who was slow, and Wayne had always been protective of him when they were little. He would never dream of being rough with a kid like that. It was something to think about. He decided he'd try giving Roach a little more time to comply after his commands.

Wayne liked that wiener dog Choco, but he wasn't sure about his owner lady. She looked uptight. He'd seen them a couple of times before. That little dog seemed to fly through the air on them stubby legs. He had Wayne's dogs running the fence until Roach was drooling. Up and down, up and down, until Thor gave up and lay down, white spittle forming at the corners of his mouth. That little hot dog had the juice, man. He never stopped.

Wayne smiled at Choco, knowing his dogs would sleep the rest of the day. He put their choke chains on them, waved at Nancy and Choco's lady, and walked his dogs back to the van. It clunked and clanked as he drove deep into the park and onto a side road, past where the campsites were, and past the area of a true road. Wayne drove straight into the tall grass and was careful to avoid making grooves where he'd driven the day before.

He parked the van, got out, and opened the side door. Thor and Roach hopped out and started sniffing the ground. They were at the edge of a fast-moving river and under a bridge where they could not be seen from the highway. It was peaceful down there. Wayne set up a folding table and took his fishing pole out. Opening a coffee can that stored his bait, he pulled out a worm and put it on the hook. Tossing his line into the river, Wayne waited.

They were a hundred miles away from where he stole the dogs, and millions of miles away from where he'd been just two years ago. Wayne had served 10 years for conspiracy to distribute weed. Just weed. Nothing else. He hadn't assaulted anyone. Wayne never held anyone at gunpoint. Wayne hadn't raped a kid. A guy who did rape several kids got out in just three years. The day that motherfucker got out, Wayne went nuts over the injustice, raging and breaking things. Wayne's cellmate tried to help by holding him down, but he'd been a smaller guy and had no chance. Wayne wound up sobbing, and a nurse had to shoot him in the ass with something to calm him. It was a couple of days in the prison mental ward for that.

While Wayne sat in jail, many states across the country legalized marijuana. Plenty of white men were now making money hand over fist selling weed from their new, legal, hipster dispensaries.

When Wayne finally got out, they gave him the clothes he'd worn into the place when he was 21. They barely fit. They gave him the change he'd had in his pocket from 10 years ago. There was no one to call. His mother, a drug addict, had never been there for him. His sister Nicky? Wayne had no idea what her phone number was now. He'd received just two letters from her while in prison, the first saying their father had died. Wayne hadn't even cared. He hated that guy for getting their mother addicted to drugs and then running off.

Wayne had a complimentary bus ticket from the prison, and without knowing for sure if she still lived there, he picked Charlotte, NC, based on the return address on Nicky's envelopes. He had 30 days to report to the parole board as to where he was living and where he was working.

Wayne watched the scenery go from back alleys and graffiti, to rural, to mountains, to city. "Welcome to Charlotte, NC," the sign read.

When he got off the bus, he was tired and hungry. A flashy-looking man in a suit coat approached asking Wayne if he needed a job. They went into a nearby diner to discuss it, and the man bought him a cheeseburger and fries. It felt like the best food Wayne had ever tasted.

The man said he needed a bouncer for his club. Wayne was a big guy, and he looked like he could do the job. The man didn't care that Wayne had just been released from prison. Chuckling, he said, "For this job, that is a bonus, my man." He would be paid under the table. No taxes. No government stuff. It wouldn't work for the parole board but would allow him to make a little money and buy some time.

The club was in an old elementary school. Wayne would find out later it was a cover for a dog-fighting ring. There was a first-floor club room with disco lights and drinks and dancing girls. Wayne desired them all but kept it professional. He needed this job, needed some money, and had to stay on task.

A bartender named Jimmy helped him track down a phone number for his sister, and she squealed with joy when she heard his voice.

"I'm out now. I'm in Charlotte. How close are you?"

"Shoot, Wayne, I used to live in Charlotte, but now I'm in Haberland City. I'm like an hour and a half, two hours from Charlotte, in *South* Carolina."

Wayne nodded, smiling wide at the sound of Nicky's voice. His sister said she was sorry for not being in touch, but she'd had two babies. Wayne now had a three-year-old nephew and five-year-old niece. Nicky's hands were full. She worked at a nursing home and had a second job waiting tables at a diner on Saturday mornings. All through nursing school, she'd worked at the diner, and the tips were too good to give up. The crew and customers had become like family to her. Wayne was so proud of her. All the shit they'd been through as kids, and Nicky had pulled herself up and out of it. A nurse now? Raising two kids on her own? Damn. He shook his head, smiling. He promised to come see her as soon as he got his money together. Wayne regretted they'd drifted apart as teenagers and wanted to make things right with his sister.

Wayne slept on a bedroll set out for him in the kitchen pantry by Jimmy the bartender. He wasn't officially supposed to be staying there, but Jimmy remembered how it felt to have nowhere to go when he got out and cleared it with The Boss, who said it was fine, just until Wayne had enough saved to rent a room somewhere.

Wayne had been bouncing in the upstairs club. When people came to the door they paid, and he stamped their hand. There was a separate stamp for those who gave him a password. If you knew the password, you got access to the basement.

The Boss watched Wayne closely for two weeks. He set up a prostitute to offer Wayne cocaine and sex. He had declined. He did not try to fuck the waitresses, and he did not engage the patrons. Wayne didn't let anyone mess with him either. He knew how to handle the occasional group of young drunk white boys and could send their balls up into their throats with a stern look.

He'd only had to lay a finger on one guy so far. A drunk college student who thought he was tough. With a one-handed shove, the kid quickly went down, and his friends scurried off with him, their adventure to the "other side of town" a story they would laugh about for years.

The Boss asked him, "How would you like to be given more responsibility?"

"And more money?" Wayne asked.

He chuckled, "Of course, my man. Of course."

"Let's do it," Wayne said.

Wayne was promoted to guarding the basement. To get there, you had to go into the main club, then out through a back door, then down a hallway and a long flight of stairs. From there, another long dark hallway took you to the doors of a room that used to be a school cafeteria. If anything looked "funny," he was to deny, even if they had the stamp. Even if they knew the password.

Wayne figured there'd be gambling, and he was right.

Standing outside the door, no one would ever know what was going on inside. Ironclad soundproofing had been installed. There was supposed to be another guy manning the door with him, but he hadn't shown up. Wayne assured The Boss he'd be okay on his own. He preferred it. Wayne hated small talk. He was so out of touch with modern society, it often felt impossible to keep up.

There was a rush of people at first, but now it was quiet in the hall. No one was coming so he cracked the door to peek at the action inside. A large crowd was gathered around a fenced ring, and people were cheering. Wayne heard dogs barking and growling. An emcee prattled on.

"This next one comes fresh from a beautiful front lawn in Eastover. Its collar, let me check. It's some kind of lap dog, maybe a Maltese? And its name is.... Princess. Of course it is!"

The crowd roared. "*Hey, Princess!*" a woman could be heard saying above the throng.

The man tossed the dog into the air, and Wayne saw a giant pit bull lunge toward it before he could slam the door shut.

He felt sick. Wayne didn't have a lot of love for rich people and their prissy pocketbook dogs, but this was not cool.

These people are fucked up, he thought.

And they were fucked up. There was every kind of drug going on in that basement. Cocaine, Heroin. Meth. Fentanyl. Molly.

Plenty of booze and hard stuff. Moonshine. Prostitutes of all shapes, sizes, and genders were servicing men in side rooms that used to be classrooms. It was what his granny would have called a sin den. She'd warned him about such places. Wayne and Nicky had lived with her out in the country when they were little. Their father had been violent, and he'd been long gone. Their mother left them with their granny when Wayne was three and Nicky was two. When Wayne was 10 years old, a boyfriend convinced their mother if she got back custody of her kids, she'd get money from the state every month. After that, he and Nicky clung to each other at night, missing their granny, while their mother shot up heroin with her scary friends in the living room of their small apartment.

Wayne and Nicky's granny cried herself to sleep every night, praying for their safety and for their return to her, which never happened. Wayne had spent another couple of days in the prison mental ward when he received Nicky's second letter telling him their granny had passed away.

Wayne heard footsteps. A couple of white guys came down the hall, showed him their stamp, and said the password. He let them in. There were all kinds here. Every race, every kind of look. Ladies in fur coats and six-inch heels. Men in hoodies. Men in suits. Men in athletic jerseys.

A couple of narcs came by, easy to spot. They were bad actors, trying to be Joe Cool. He told them this was a private party, and they had the wrong place. They asked about dog fights, and Wayne told them he'd heard there were some happening across town at a made-up address. They left.

The Boss came through the door to check on him. He tried to read Wayne's face. Was he seeing something?

Wayne gave nothing away.

"They want the dogs to taste blood before the fight, you see. It makes them want it. Makes them thirsty."

Wayne said nothing. Nodded once.

"We usually give them four or five as bait, to get 'em going before the real fights."

Wayne remained stone-faced.

The Boss nodded and smiled, happy Wayne wasn't going to be a problem.

Wayne asked him to cover for him while he went to take a piss. The Boss lit a cigarette and said, "Sure, but make it quick. I have a lot to tend to in there," offering a broad Cheshire Cat smile.

Walking down the long hall to the bathroom, Wayne passed a row of empty cat carriers. He guessed one had been for the little white dog. Another carrier held two puppies. They looked to be no more than 10 pounds each. One was black with little beige spots where his eyebrows would be. The other was light brown. They'd been huddled together, but when he passed, they began to whine and cry, pawing at the metal door of the carrier.

Wayne went into the restroom. He stood with one hand on the wall above the urinal, holding himself steady.

He'd seen all kinds of shit in prison. He'd seen guys get their faces punched in, and otherwise get the shit truly kicked out of them. One time, he saw a guy pummeled with a lock in a sock for narcing. Why was he giving a damn about these puppies about to get eaten alive for these whacked-out motherfuckers' entertainment? Who cared?

But he did care.

He looked in the mirror as he washed his hands.

Perhaps it was because he'd seen so much violence and injustice. He'd had enough of it all. He'd become hard, had to, but this felt like a turning point. It was his chance to stay human.

On the way out of the bathroom, he picked up the carrier with the two puppies and headed out the back exit. The solid metal door clanked shut behind him, locking him out of the dog fights forever.

Walking away from the place, he remembered who he was. He was his granny's. He was his sister's. He wanted no part in killing puppies. He wasn't going back to that sin den. He was not going to risk a bust and get sent back to prison. Fuck that shit.

Wayne walked for hours with the puppies in the carrier, not knowing where he would go or what he would do, or if the Boss would find him and kill him. How big of a transgression was this?

Either way, it was done. This was it. A new story.

Wayne and the puppies slept in the woods that night. The next morning, he stood on the side of the road, carrying one puppy in the crate, the other under his arm, sticking his thumb out to every passing car. A young man in a Jeep pulled over, and Wayne told him he'd been transporting the puppies across state lines to their new owner when his car broke down. The Jeep took Wayne all the way to Haberland City. On the ride, Wayne told the guy he'd forgotten his phone in his car, and the young man let him use his cell to call Nicky. He'd memorized her number.

Wayne stayed on Nicky's couch. She got him a job washing dishes at the diner to keep the parole board off his back. Her kids were in heaven over the puppies, but they lived in a studio apartment that didn't allow pets, and the puppies weren't housebroken. After a month, the whole situation was testing Nicky's nerves. And then, one Saturday afternoon, she came home from her shift at the diner with a surprise for him. A gift from Bob, one of her regular customers.

Bob was in his seventies and had been coming to the diner for years. He showed up at 11 a.m. every Saturday like clockwork. He ordered a beet salad and an iced tea. Bob lived close by and walked to the diner from his apartment. He always tipped well, but Nicky never would have guessed how wealthy he truly was. She also didn't realize he noticed how hard she worked, and admired how diplomatic she was with customers. Bob was impressed with how Nicky put herself through school to become an LPN while working at the diner and raising two children on her own. He knew she hadn't gotten a fair shake in life and felt if Nicky had the same opportunities he'd had, she'd probably be CEO of her own company by now. He rooted for Nicky, the way one might for a favorite niece. They'd had many conversations over the years, with Bob mostly listening, sometimes embarrassed by his own good fortune.

The story of her brother Wayne particularly moved him. Marijuana was now legal in many states, and Bob himself benefited from it greatly for his arthritis. His son lived in Florida where medical marijuana was easy to get, and kept him supplied. Even though weed wasn't legal in SC, Bob's freezer was full of it, and he knew he'd never spend a day in jail if he were caught with it. He could afford the right attorneys. He could afford bail.

Bob never shared with Nicky that he used marijuana—that would be cruel—but her heartache over her brother all those years tugged at his conscience.

Bob watched Wayne doing dishes without complaint. He could see Nicky was going out of her mind cramped in that apartment but knew she was too proud to take money from him, and Wayne would likely be the same. So, he bought a van from a junkyard. Keeping the outside rough, he had the engine replaced and asked the mechanic to rig the muffler to sound a bit clunky. He fitted it with a mattress. He took it to the diner that Saturday and casually offered it to Nicky.

"I've had it forever, and wouldn't get a dime for it anyway," he told her, taking a long drink of iced tea through his straw. "Maybe you could sell it for parts," he said, setting his empty glass down on the counter.

Bob led Nicky outside behind the diner and showed her the van. It didn't look like anything special. She noted the mattress in the back. He told her he'd used it for camping.

Bob said, "You'll be saving me from having to pay a junkman to come get it. Honestly, you're doing me a favor if you take it."

He closed the van door and shrugged like it didn't matter to him one way or the other and handed her the keys.

Wayne still used Nicky's mailing address but had been living in the van down by the river for almost two years. After his six months of parole were up, he stopped working at the diner, and began living off the grid.

Wayne's granny had taught them to fish and grow food. He kept himself, the dogs, and Nicky's family in fresh seafood, mostly trout. Wayne also kept a few plants down by the river. Potatoes, tomatoes, greens. A small garden in five-gallon buckets, easily moved into the van or hidden in tall grasses if he needed to go quickly. Standing in the river up to his knees in the cool water, fishing line bobbing gently in the breeze, Wayne was sometimes almost moved to tears at the freedom. The pure cold running water. The sound of the birds. The blue sky, the fresh open air. No fences holding him in. It felt like paradise.

Wayne bathed in the river in the warm months. In winter he took sponge baths. Sometimes he'd take a long hot shower at Nicky's. Laundry was a different issue. It was difficult getting to a laundromat with the dogs, so he sometimes had to wear the same dirty clothes for a week. He'd rinse his underwear in the river and hang them on the side mirrors of the van to dry, but it wasn't the same clean a washing machine provided.

The dogs made it hard to find a real job, but they were doing okay. They had what they needed. Wayne did odd jobs, including detailing cars at pop-up shops that happened in the park on a regular basis. It paid for the little gas money he required. Occasionally, he'd work as a bouncer at a local club.

Exercise had kept him sane when he was in prison, so he'd finagled a weight workout using gallon jugs filled with different levels of water. He also used the outdoor workout equipment and obstacle course in the park at night. Wayne knew security patrolled at 11 p.m. and again at 3 a.m. so the place was pretty much all his otherwise. There was a homeless community in tents in the woods, but they all stuck to themselves at the other end of the park. There might be safety in numbers, but Wayne preferred solitude.

At night, the moon would shine on the rushing water. Wayne had freedom to walk around and breathe and stretch and look up at the stars. No one told him what to do. No one was looking down on him. There was the occasional car traveling over the bridge at night, but no sounds of inmates screaming, or cell doors clunking or rattling. The absence of those sounds was something Wayne would never take for granted.

Taking off his outer layers of clothing, Wayne looked at Thor and Roach asleep on the mattress. How did he get here, in this creaky van in the woods with these two crazy dogs? Why had he spent 10 years in prison *for weed?* He'd been just a kid. Wayne felt that familiar prickle of self-pity, then shook himself out of it. He knew from experience it was a dangerous road leading nowhere. He prayed, not to God, but to his granny, and felt her presence, protecting him. Wayne hoped she was proud of him. He'd kept his dignity inside that place. He'd never ratted anyone out, kept his nose clean. He'd *minded his own goddamn business* like she'd taught him. Wayne climbed onto the mattress and settled in between the giant dogs. Roach picked up his head and with adoring eyes slapped a sloppy tongue across Wayne's face. Wayne smiled, tousled Roach's head, and said, "Hopefully that little hot dog will be there for you to run with tomorrow," then flipped on his side before surrendering to sleep.

CHAPTER 7

The Irritating Sound of Chatter

When Ann and Choco arrived at the dog park, Nancy waved like they were old friends. "Come on in, Ann!"

Teddy stood up to greet Choco. He sniffed his butt and his mouth then heaved himself back down at Nancy's feet. A petite round gray pit bull who looked more like a baby hippo than a dog ran over to greet them. Choco barked and wagged his tail, and they ran circles around each other, yapping. The pit bull's tail was docked, and its little nub wagged excitedly.

A young woman who'd been walking laps came over and, smiling at Choco, asked, "Who's this little doggo?" She wore leggings, sneakers, and a long-sleeved crop top that exposed her midriff and fit tight across the chest. Her brown hair had chunky blonde highlights, and she wore it in a high ponytail. She came to the dog park with a full face of makeup, including eyebrows and lashes.

Nancy answered for Ann. "This is Choco! Isn't he a cute little guy? And he's so friendly! Who doesn't like a hot dog?" she said, scratching Choco behind the ears.

Nancy said, "Trish, this is Ann."

Ann replied, "Nice to meet you."

Trish smiled and said, "Same."

Trish sat down, and Choco put his paws up on her lap. She giggled and picked him up, nuzzling his face.

"You *are* a friendly little thing, aren't you?" Choco leaned in as she cooed at him. Her long, manicured fingernails scritchy-scratched down the length of his back.

Ann smiled, used to Choco getting attention wherever he went. Glancing at the little gray pit bull, she asked, "Is this one yours?"

Trish nodded, saying, "This is Gigi. Also known as Gorgeous Girl! She's a rescue. I don't know who rescued who, though," bowing her head and moving it reverently side to side.

Ann tried not to roll her eyes at the overused expression. She'd been leery of pit bulls, but it was evident Gigi was harmless as she lay on her back, rolling side to side, smiling with her Joker-like jaws. Choco jumped down from Trish's lap and offered Gigi a play-bow. Gigi hopped up and began happily prancing with him across the green space.

Wayne had just arrived, and Gigi and Choco joined his dogs in a game of run-the-fence. The giant dogs on the outside, the smaller dogs on the inside chasing them like shadows. Choco ran like a dog possessed, ears flapping, oblivious to the fact he was almost 10 years old. Whatever mechanism most dogs had that signaled them to stop, Choco seemed to lack. He had always been this way playing with toys as well. He'd run after his green ball for hours if someone would keep throwing it to him. Ann sometimes forced Liam to stop, fearful Choco would drop dead of a heart attack.

Trish prattled on about *The Kardashians*, *The Bachelor*, and her very favorite reality show, *Pit Bulls and Parolees*. Nancy nodded along, adding her two cents where she could.

Another young woman wearing a Hello Kitty backpack and noise-canceling headphones entered the gazebo and sat down. She took off the headphones but did not contribute to the conversation and did not make eye contact with any of them.

Nancy said, "Hello, my name is Nancy."

The woman parroted, in the exact same tone, "Hello, my name is Nancy."

Nancy said, "Your name is Nancy too?"

"No, I'm Iris," the young woman said.

Confusion washed over Nancy's face. Trish studied Iris for a moment, furrowing her brow.

Just then, a fire engine sounded, and Iris covered her ears with her hands. She began to rock.

Ann didn't want to hear about *The Kardashians* or any other reality shows. She thought of them as junk food for the brain and had no patience for those who would fill themselves up on them. Not when there were so many books to read that could actually enrich a person.

She also didn't know what this girl Iris's issue was, but she couldn't deal with it today. Normally, Ann would be the first one to offer compassion, but instead she pulled her keys out of her purse. Enough with the chatter. Enough with the noise!

Trish noticed the Florida Atlantic University keychain Ann held in her hand. "Are you an FAU mom? My best friend from elementary school went there!"

"My son," Ann said, a lump forming in her throat. She didn't want to talk about Liam. Not now. Not with this young woman.

Trish continued, "Would you believe she blocked me? Totally ghosted me, and I've known her since fifth grade!"

"I've known her since fifth grade!" Iris repeated.

Nancy glanced at Iris, then back to Trish, saying, "I blocked my best friend a few years ago. And my ex-husband too. They can both go straight to hell."

Trish, Ann, and Iris all raised their eyebrows, but Nancy didn't elaborate. She took out a pack of Salem Lights, tapped it on her thigh several times, and then lit a cigarette, blowing her smoke in the opposite direction of the others, lost in her own thoughts.

Trish began talking again. The sound of her chatter left Ann feeling irritated and exhausted. She said goodbye and clicked Choco's leash onto his collar. In the car he circled three times on the passenger seat before lying down. She rested her hand on Choco's back and noticed the appearance of some white fur around his muzzle. Ann felt hot and shaky. The thought of him getting old, the thought of losing Choco one day too? It was too much.

The car was still in park, and she rolled down her window for air. She gripped the steering wheel with both hands and began the breathing exercises her therapist had taught her.

Breathing in, two... three... four.

Breathing out, two... three... four... five... six.

A few rounds in, she noticed the father and daughter with the huskies pull into the parking lot once again.

The daughter got out of the passenger's side with the younger dog. Her jaw was set, and she wore a scowl on her face. Her outfit was black skinny jeans, black Converse sneakers, and a David Bowie t-shirt. Ann smiled. The child liked David Bowie? It had always amused her the way Liam's generation thought they had discovered the music of Ann's youth. She herself had seen Bowie in concert four times.

As they walked toward the enclosures, the girl held the leash with both hands as the young dog pulled her across the parking lot. The other two dogs once again walked calmly beside her father. Ann noticed father and daughter had the same thick straight dark hair and long Roman noses. He walked with his chest puffed out, and yelled over his shoulder, "Jesus Christ, Becky, how many times do I have to tell you not to let him drag you?"

When he turned his back to her, Becky once again gave him the finger. It seemed to be her signature move.

Ann couldn't help but chuckle to herself.

As the three huskies entered the large-dog section, Ann noticed a young couple frantically calling their Irish setter.

"Otis! Otis!"

The huskies ran straight toward the dog, who flipped on its back exposing its belly, submitting. The man and woman hurried toward them, and the woman clapped her hands at the huskies, who then scattered.

They quickly gathered their dog to leave, and as they passed Ann's car in the parking lot, she heard them talking. "He says it's only playing, but that is *not* playing. He snarls. His growl is unnerving," the woman said.

"The two older huskies are fine, but there's something wrong with the younger dog," the man added.

Watching the scene unfold, Ann realized the near panic she'd been feeling had subsided.

Her therapist was right. The dog park was serving as a distraction. The breathing exercises were helping. Once again, she placed her hand on Choco's back. She closed her eyes and felt his ribs move in and out with his breath, her body calming further. Choco seemed not to have a care in the world. Ann wished she could live in the present like dogs did. It would be so much easier than living with a constant flood of memories, when even the good ones hurt. It would be so much easier than living with the dread of every tomorrow unfolding without Liam. Earlier, she'd almost told Nancy about his accident, but had been unable to get the words out. She didn't feel like talking about Liam with Trish there. She just seemed so shallow. Though, of course, Ann hardly knew her.

CHAPTER 8

Trish

Trish spent the better part of her twenties in love with a man named Tyler who would never love her back romantically. It wasn't that he didn't want to. She worked as a hair stylist, and they met when he came in for a fade. Everyone thought they were the perfect couple. Tyler went as far as proposing when Trish was 27. After dating for five years, he had been getting a lot of pressure from Trish, and also his family, to pop the question.

Trish always thought by the time she was 30 she'd have two kids, possibly three, but Tyler had been taking his sweet time. He finally asked her to marry him on her birthday, after a fancy dinner at a rooftop restaurant downtown. The ring was placed perfectly atop a piece of chocolate cake. Trish cried and said, "Yes. Of course I will marry you!" before jumping into his arms.

For two blissful weeks, Trish obsessively looked through wedding magazines, dog-earing pages and circling ideas with a

Sharpie. She smiled dreamily, thinking of walking down the aisle in a white dress toward Tyler.

It was the finality of the engagement that propelled Tyler to admit to himself, and to Trish, he was gay.

Looking back, Trish conceded there had been signs. They were both fans, but Tyler knew the choreography to Britney Spears's "Oops, I Did It Again" better than Trish did. Upon further reflection, she also had to admit his obsession with the TV show *Glee* should have been a clue.

It also hadn't gone unnoticed to Trish how the male stylists often eyed Tyler when he visited her at work, but she'd thought nothing of it. Women did the same. After all, Tyler was an exceptionally attractive man, and dapper, too. He worked as a bank teller and often wore suits in pastel colors with pocket squares, and wing-tipped Italian leather shoes on his feet. Trish had thought he looked like a hipster, not gay.

And of course, there was the sex. Tyler never initiated, but after dating men who *always* wanted sex, this seemed like a relief. Trish was beautiful and had always received unwanted attention from men. Tyler had been different, and she convinced herself he was just being a gentleman, letting her take the lead.

Of course, Trish still loved Tyler. He couldn't help being gay. She held him in her arms all weekend after he told her. *Her* dreams were dashed, but she comforted *him*. She was worried about him. He was so ashamed. She stroked his hair and told him it was okay. He needed to be who he was. She thanked him for telling her the truth.

Trish had spent five years of her life thinking he was "the one," but forgave him instantly for breaking her heart.

What she didn't expect was for Tyler to run off with a man less than a month later and post it all over social media. Tyler was finally "out," and proud, but Trish felt humiliated.

The first few months, she sat in her apartment in a daze whenever she wasn't at work. The next few months, she began scrolling online dating sites. She wasn't ready to meet anyone but felt the need to see what was out there. Swipe, swipe, swipe. Trish was suspicious of all of them. She got a lot of requests but didn't reply to any of them.

One Friday after work, Trish changed into pajamas and started in on a jumbo bag of Doritos. She flipped through the channels and found herself watching a 48-hour marathon of *Pit Bulls and Parolees*. Trish had never considered getting a dog before, but suddenly needed one, and not just any dog, a pit bull!

For two weeks, she found herself scrolling through Petfinder with much more enthusiasm than she'd had for online dating. When she saw Gigi's face, *she knew.*

Trish barely slept Sunday night worrying the little gray pit bull she'd fallen in love with might already be spoken for. Monday morning, she called the rescue, and to her great relief, the dog that had stolen her heart was still available!

Trish knew she'd have to pay a pet fee each month on top of her rent. She was having a hard time paying her bills already since Tyler left. Trish was also surprised how expensive it was to adopt, even from a rescue, but she put it on her credit card. After all, this was a *soul* she was trying to save. It was important.

In the year since adopting Gigi, Trish had become a zealot about the breed. She talked about it with clients as she cut and colored their hair. Her coworkers' eyes had begun to glaze over whenever she got on her pit bull soapbox. "Sorry, not sorry," Trish would say, after delivering an unsolicited lecture.

In line at the grocery store, Trish sang the praises of pit bulls, showing pictures of Gigi to the cashier. She even gave a public service announcement to the gynecologist during her pelvic exam, and proudly left that day with a refill on her birth control (she had not given up all hope) and the peace of mind that came with teaching one more skeptic about this misunderstood breed.

At 28, Trish's dreams of marriage seemed far away, but having Gigi in her life served as balm to her soul. Trish decided she didn't need a man. She would focus on herself, and her dog. She began taking Gigi to Lake Woof a couple of times a week. And then one day, a shirtless Tommy ran up, dancing, singing, and glistening with sweat. When she saw the pit bull attached to the leash he was holding, it was as if the heavens parted. Unfortunately, she would soon find out he had a girlfriend.

CHAPTER 9

Balls and Apples,
and Melons

Choco ran the fence with Thor and Roach. Ed and Tommy finished their laps and stopped to chat with Nancy and the others in the gazebo. They were talking about Tommy's dog Rocky, who was infamously intact. Rocky, named after the main character in Tommy's favorite movie of all time, was already 70 pounds. Less than a year ago, Tommy found the tiny pit bull mix wandering by a dumpster at a music festival. Tommy played guitar in high school and had been asked by a friend to fill in for a local band when their guitarist got sick that day. He'd just finished the set when he found Rocky. Tommy teared up whenever he talked about how baby Rocky's ribs were showing through his skin, and how he was trying to eat an empty catsup packet the first time he saw him.

"He was starving, y'all," he'd say, shaking his head solemnly. His voice had a Southern drawl reminiscent of a young Matthew McConaughey.

"Doesn't he sound like the guy from *Magic Mike?*" Trish asked Ann, Nancy, and Iris one day as they'd watched Tommy head toward the gate with Rocky. Ann didn't know. She hadn't seen *Magic Mike*, a film about male strippers.

Nancy said, "Yeah, I see it."

Iris nodded, looking down at her Mary Jane shoes. Her dog Buster was busy chasing squirrels at the far end of the park. Iris blushed, thinking of the movie, and pushed her pink-framed glasses back up onto the bridge of her nose. She cleared her throat. "I would say he does," Iris said.

Becky was sitting next to Trish. Bruce had dropped her off at Lake Woof saying he had errands to run, but she suspected he was going to Malone's Tavern. Bruce said he'd be an hour, but it had already been three. The huskies were at the far end of the park, lying down in the grass. They were no doubt hungry. Neither they nor Becky had eaten dinner.

Tommy said his girlfriend was away visiting her sister the weekend he brought Rocky home. He locked the puppy in the bathroom before leaving for work the next morning. Tommy did rotating shifts at the local hospital as a transporter, pushing patients to and from surgeries and procedures. All day long, he'd chat with patients, joking with them, getting them from point A to point B feeling a little more comfortable and less afraid. He loved nothing more than to tell a story, and all his patients got an earful that day about the puppy waiting for him in the bathroom at home.

After work, he cleaned up the mess the little guy had made in the bathroom and gave him a bath. He fed him. All evening, he rehearsed his list of "pros" to convince his girlfriend, whom he affectionately referred to as his "lady," that they should keep the puppy. Tommy's lady worked as a unit secretary at the same hospital he worked at and was studying to become a respiratory therapist. When she got home, she took one look at Rocky, and shook her head, doubtfully. Tommy braced himself for the inevitable no.

She knelt and petted the squirming pup, all clean and fluffy from his bath, and said, "He *is* pretty cute." She stood up, looked Tommy in the eye, and said, "As long as you take care of him, I don't mind. But he's not going to be *my* problem."

"Fair enough!" Tommy said, throwing his arms around her and kissing her on the mouth.

Now, Rocky was huge and all muscle. His thick head and jaws gave away his pit bull status. His brown striped coat was short, still puppy soft. And now, his testicles were big enough to affect his gait. They were a topic of discussion at the dog park, and everywhere else it seemed. Around town, all eyes were on Rocky's balls. Some folks would stare blatantly. The more proper Southern ladies averted their glances, but no one could resist taking a peek, getting an eyeful.

Any time someone kindly suggested getting him neutered, Tommy would shudder, imagining his own testicles being cut off, and his hands would instinctively fly to his crotch for protection.

"They don't hack 'em off with a machete, Tommy," Nancy said now. "They use a scalpel with surgical precision. They numb 'em, Tommy. The dogs don't feel a thing."

Nancy turned to Iris.

"Buster is neutered, right?"

Iris again looked at the ground but nodded. "Yes, Buster did okay with it."

Tommy shook his head.

"And the huskies?" she asked, looking at Becky. "They're all boys, right?'

Becky nodded.

"What about *after*, Nancy? How is he supposed to feel after?" Tommy pleaded.

Nancy looked at Ed. "Your dog is fixed, right?"

Ed responded, "Henry came to me that way when I took him in after my neighbor died."

Nancy cupped her hands around her mouth and shouted to Wayne, who was walking along the outside of the fence toward his van with Thor and Roach, "What about your boys, Wayne? Are they neutered?"

"Yeah, my sister set that up for me when we were staying with her," he called back as he got in the van and drove off. He wondered why they were asking but shrugged and let it go.

Tommy wasn't going to admit the real reason he was dragging his feet. The real reason was he was afraid of blood. He was afraid of seeing the stitches after the procedure. Any time he pushed a wheelchair into a patient's room and saw they were in the middle of a blood draw, or a dressing change, he felt he might faint. He'd wait outside the patient's room with his back against the wall, his skin clammy and white, breathing deeply until everything was bandaged up and good to go. Whenever he passed phlebotomists in the hospital hallways rolling their carts with vials of blood, he looked the other way. The phlebotomists had mistakenly pegged him as unfriendly, though nothing could have been further from the truth.

The thought of Rocky's testicles being cut off, even under anesthesia, was too much for Tommy.

"I can't do that to my boy," he said. "It's inhumane!"

No one at the dog park knew Tommy's girlfriend's name, but everyone knew he was crazy about her. He practically burst with pride, telling everyone how she was crushing it in school. For months, he worked extra shifts saving money to buy her a new used car just to make her life easier.

Trish listened to Tommy talk about her. Dreamily, she hoped one day someone would love her the way Tommy loved his girlfriend. She wished someone would be proud of her and call her their "lady." She thought Tommy was probably the perfect boyfriend. Plus, he had a pit bull.

Tommy would say something like, "What do you think about Rock's new collar? My lady got it for him." Then he'd reach down to scratch Rocky behind the ears. "She has great taste, right? Mommy takes good care of us, right, Rocky?"

Trish would sigh.

Gretchen, a tall imposing woman, the self-appointed deputy of the dog park, entered the gazebo. "What's your *lady* think about getting him fixed?" she asked, eyes on Rocky's testicles, not knowing the topic had already been covered for the day.

Gretchen always arrived with four rescue dogs whom she paid no attention to, feeling their behavior would always be above par. She chose to focus instead on what the other dog owners were doing wrong. She wore her hair in two long dark braids, always. On her feet were hiking boots all year round, and a shoestring held a whistle around her neck that she didn't hesitate to use whenever dogs got into scuffles. Gretchen patrolled the park, reminding people to pick up their dog poops. She gave unsolicited advice on dog behavior and discipline, and tried hard to recruit people to her dog training classes at the community center.

Gretchen despised the idea of unneutered dogs in the park. She felt the only thing worse was when *some fool* would bring a female dog in heat.

"He gets out and gets another dog pregnant, you'll have trouble on your hands. The shelters are always full, you know."

"Don't worry, Gretchen. I keep a good eye on ole Rocky boy. He ain't gonna knock anyone up," Tommy said, flashing her a wide grin that worked with most women.

Uncharmed, Gretchen continued, "That's what people always say, but then the shelters have to euthanize the unwanted puppies that come when people are reckless."

"I'll keep that in mind, Gretchen," Tommy said, diplomatically. "I'll be careful," he added, once again imagining the blood, shuddering, and quickly dismissing the idea.

"So, you'll make an appointment, Tommy? Plain and simple, it's irresponsible not to," she pressed.

Finally, Tommy blurted, "He's *my* dog, and my girlfriend says what we do with him is up to me. She made it clear his balls are none of her business, so I don't see how they're *your* business. She also says, as long as he's not humping the shit out of everything he sees, it's not a problem for her, and I don't see why it's a problem for *you*."

Ann glanced over at Nancy. They shared a smile.

Nancy changed the subject. "So how *is* your lady, Tommy?"

Tommy closed his eyes and shook his head. "Oh my God, Nance, you're never gonna believe this one. Her mother is visiting from Columbia—I think I told you that. She doesn't like dogs, but what are you gonna do? We have the extra bedroom and what can we say, *no*? It was supposed to be for just a week. She won't stay longer because she don't like ole Rocky."

He stopped to pet Rocky. "What'd you ever do to her? Right, Rocky, ole boy? It's not your fault. Who doesn't like my Rock?"

Drool hung down from both sides of Rocky's mouth. His big Joker-like jaws smiled up at Tommy. He leaned in as Tommy scratched behind his ears. "Who's a good boy? You are. Right, Rock?"

Tommy patted Rocky on the rump and continued, "So, our apartment isn't exactly soundproof. And my lady ain't gonna give me none with her mother in the next room. And I can't say as I blame her because we can get a little *loud.* I mean," he put his hand to the side of his lips as if whispering, "she's kind of an animal."

Nancy chuckled.

"Okay, Tommy, we get it. Spare us the details," Gretchen said.

Iris stared at the ground, smiling, and said, "She's kind of an animal," under her breath, then pushed her glasses back up onto the bridge of her nose. She was enjoying being included in these conversations.

"Well, this morning, I walk into our bedroom, and I see my lady there in her bathrobe, and I know she ain't got nothing on underneath it. She only wears it after her shower, before she gets dressed, and only wears it when we have guests. Usually, she's just fine walking around butt naked. But anyway, it's got big flowers on it. Not really my style, but what's underneath it is what counts, and it kinda gets me going."

Ed, glancing at the women, asked, "Is this story appropriate to tell in mixed company, Tommy?"

Nancy laughed, "Oh give me a break, Ed. We can take it."

Ed glanced at Becky.

Becky, rolling her eyes, said, "I'm not *a child,*" even though at 14 she technically still was.

Now Tommy had the whole group's attention. He paused, raised an eyebrow, and continued.

"So, she's leaning over, fishing for something from the bottom of the closet, and I am *overcome with desire*. I sneak up behind, wrap my arms around, and grab hold of her boobs."

Tommy gestured with both hands, like he had a grip on two melons. He continued, "And I say, in a whisper—because Tommy don't want to be rude, don't want her ma to hear—I say, I can't take it much longer. I gotta have you soon, baby."

He stopped, put his index finger and thumb to his chin for a beat, then back to melon hands.

"At this point," he said, "I notice, somethin's funny. Somethin's *off*."

He shook his head, furrowing his brow,

"*These* ain't my lady's tatas. They feel... different? My lady's got cute little apples, and these are like honeydews, ya know? What I've got in my hands are not only bigger but not as perky. I mean, they aren't bad—there's no such thing as bad boobs, am I right? But these were bigger and softer."

He scanned the group, left to right. Nancy's jaw dropped. Ed's eyes went wide. Iris was looking at her feet. Becky looked from Tommy to Nancy, her mouth agape.

"And now that I'm thinking about it, this ass I'm pressing up against, this ain't her ass either!"

"No!" Nancy howled.

The group erupted in laughter. Ed began shaking his head. Nancy slapped her thigh, saying, "Tommy, no!"

Looking point-blank at her, Tommy replied, "Nancy, yes."

Iris said, "Nancy, yes," then snorted loudly as she giggled, causing the group to erupt in even more laughter.

Trish and Becky looked at each other, laughing so hard, tears streamed down their faces.

Tommy dropped his head, looked at the ground, and shuddered before continuing, "I've got my hands on my lady's *ma's* boobs, and I freeze, man. I mean, I actually freeze. I can't take them off. I can't move. I don't know what to do."

He made a display of flinging his hands in the air,

"Finally, I let go, and I backed off like a criminal trying to convince the cops not to shoot."

Grabbing his hair with both hands, he paced the gazebo.

"And now, she ain't lookin' at me. She shakes it off like she's got the willies. I try to apologize—Ma, I'm sorry! Ma, I thought you were Gina!"

It was the first time the group had heard Gina's actual name.

"And she says two words: 'I'm aware.'"

A pause.

"Her ma didn't speak to me the rest of the morning, and I couldn't wait to get out of the house and bring ole Rocky here today."

Trish pondered what it would feel like to have Tommy's hands on her own breasts. She wondered what he would think of hers and did a quick self-assessment. She was somewhere between apples and honeydews. Right in the middle.

"Now my lady, she's texting me, her ma says she's going home today. She's cutting her visit short. Gina wants to know what happened."

He added, "I don't want to be around when she finds out. It ain't gonna be pretty, I tell ya that much. She says I'm always doing somethin' stupid."

Tommy shook his head and sat down on the bench across from Ann and Nancy.

Rocky, Choco, and Gigi ran over to the tree to see what Iris's dog Buster was barking about, then up the dirt mountain before looping back to the gazebo. Choco put his paws on Nancy's lap, and she picked him up.

Just when the laughter had settled down a bit, Tommy shuddered again, holding his hands out in front of him.

"I can't get the feel of her boobs off my fingers!"

Even Gretchen couldn't help but laugh.

That evening, Becky was missing her mother. She took out her sketch pad and tried to draw Katie but was having difficulty remembering her exact face. When it didn't come out right, she tore out the sketch and crumpled it up. Instead, she began drawing a portrait of Tommy and Rocky. The next week, she drew Nancy. In time, she'd get to all the Lake Woof regulars, and then, all of their dogs.

CHAPTER 10

A Puppy, Out of Spite

After school one day, Becky stood in the bathroom mirror, looking for some sign of Katie in herself, but all she saw in her reflection was Bruce. His hair. His nose. She was starting to forget Katie's voice. Everyone had always said Katie had the best laugh, but Becky couldn't remember the sound of it. She had nothing of her mother's to grab onto. She had no photos and hadn't seen her little brothers since Katie's funeral. Evan offered to drive the four hours to pick her up and have her stay the weekend with them, but Bruce had firmly said no. He'd also refused to let Katie's parents take her back to Florida with them for a week when they'd offered. They sent her cards sometimes, but she had not seen her grandparents since Katie died.

There was so much Becky didn't know about her parents. Bruce and Katie had divorced when she was a baby. They'd married when both were just 19, and though she wasn't pregnant at the time, Becky would arrive within a year. Bruce had been a high school football star and wrestling champion and was competitive to the core. The local newspaper often featured him on the sports page. He was going places, they'd said. This kid might make it pro!

Katie was a bubbly blond cheerleader, and she'd set her sights on Bruce. When they started dating, she was so chatty she often didn't notice he wasn't talking at all. Katie loved people. She loved parties. She adored attention, and carried Bruce socially without realizing she was doing it. What Katie didn't love was school. She wanted no part of going to college.

Rage bubbled just beneath Bruce's surface, and his only outlets for that rage were the high school football field and wrestling mats. One time, he'd tackled another player hard enough to ruin the kid's career. The boy, just 17 years old, needed surgery and would never play football again.

Bruce shrugged it off, saying, "All's fair in love and war." His lack of empathy for the other teenage athlete confused Katie, but she brushed it off, figuring she didn't know much about sports mindsets.

Although she was smart, academics had not come easy for Katie. Numbers and letters often flickered and flipped on the page, seemingly playing tricks on her, making her feel dumb. She wanted nothing more than to marry Bruce and become a mommy. Her parents were not happy with the plan.

Bruce's father had not finished high school and did not show up for Bruce's graduation, choosing instead to sit home in the dark getting drunk. Bruce and his mother and younger brother got home from the ceremony to find his father eager to pick a fight with the new graduate.

"Now you think you're better than me?" his father slurred.

Bruce, for the first time ever, stood up to him, answering, "I don't think it, I *know* it."

His mother stood by meekly when his father started swinging at Bruce, but this time Bruce hit back, bloodying his father's mouth. Outraged, his father called Bruce a "mouthy little bitch" and a "loser" and told him to find another place to live, officially kicking Bruce out of the house and out of the family.

Bruce stayed at the YMCA for a few weeks and tried to contact his mother and his brother, but neither would talk to him. They'd been forbidden. Fuck both of them, he thought. Katie was the only one he had.

Football dreams took a back seat to survival, and Bruce took a job at a local warehouse, unloading pallets to pay for rent. It didn't take much convincing for him to marry Katie. Things were good at first. They were playing house, and a few months later, she was pregnant with Becky. Her parents gave them money for a down payment on a small house they could barely afford. Katie set it up, decorated, and made it nice.

Becky was just a few months old when Bruce started getting rough with Katie. They'd have the smallest of fights, and suddenly, he'd be on her, pinning her to the wall. Twice he'd smashed his fist into the wall just beside her head. He didn't know what came over him in these moments, but she pissed him off so bad. She was always telling him what he needed to do: Mow the lawn. Help me with these dishes. Can you please take the baby? Can you pick up diapers? Formula? Can you please pick up your socks? Her lists went on and on. She treated him like a child, or a slave. His mother had done all that stuff herself, and he didn't know why he was supposed to do Katie's work for her.

He was overwhelmed and resentful with the responsibility of paying rent and all the other bills to support Katie and the baby. Didn't she see that? He never got to do anything fun anymore. No football. No wrestling. There was no thrill from training, or from winning anything. No one acted like he was a big deal anymore.

Bruce worked all day at the warehouse lifting heavy boxes in 100-degree heat with no air conditioning; in the winter it would be freezing. Katie didn't seem to care how hard he worked. There was no praise for the football star, only, "Baby, the light bill is due."

Bruce shoved her twice. He'd raised his hand to hit her once but stopped himself. He also picked up a vase one time and threw it at the wall, just missing her head. Katie cried about that fucking vase for days.

But that baby. That Becky. He loved her so. Bruce called her his "diamond." His prize. The love he felt for her the first time he held her almost knocked him over. Bruce knew in an instant he would die for her. He loved her more than anything he'd ever loved in the world. Much more than he loved Katie. Even so, he would hand the baby over to Katie the second he smelled a dirty diaper.

Shortly before Becky's second birthday, Katie brought up the idea of getting a puppy.

"C'mon, baby. It would be so nice for Becky to grow up with a dog. Her own little pet. Wouldn't it be great to get her a puppy for her birthday? The lady down the road, her husky had puppies a couple weeks ago, and they are so cute! You always said you liked the breed. They need homes, and I think it would be a great idea."

"No!" Bruce bellowed, surprised by his own anger. "I don't need one more thing to take care of. I never get a minute to do anything fun as it is. I never get to hang out with my friends."

"What friends?" Katie asked derisively. All his football friends had gone to college. He had no friends, other than her.

The veins in his neck bulged, and his eyes opened wide, then drew into a squint, losing their human quality. She recognized "the look" and quickly put Becky in her Exersaucer, then ran toward the bedroom, steering Bruce away from their child.

Bruce was on her in an instant, pinning her to the wall in the hallway with one hand around her throat; the other came down in a hard slap on the side of her face. Katie felt her teeth rattle. Bruce raised his hand again. "You think it's funny speaking to me that way?" Once again, he brought his palm down heavy across Katie's cheek.

Katie saw stars and felt pain in her jaw. He let go of her, and she dropped to the floor where she curled into a fetal position and began to sob.

Bruce stood over her, shaking with a rage he didn't understand. He tried to make his brain say she made him do it, but knew it wasn't true. He'd felt rage on the football field, and on the wrestling mat plenty of times, even used it as fuel, but he'd never hit a girl before. He'd always said he never would, but in a matter of seconds, he'd just crossed his own line, twice.

Bruce stomped past Becky, who was now shrieking, and out of the house. He got in his truck and sped out of the driveway, tires spitting gravel, a plume of dust in his wake. He drove for an hour going 90 MPH with heavy metal music blasting. Finally, he circled back toward town and pulled into Malone's Tavern, where the regulars ordered the high school football legend drink after drink. Soon they convinced him he'd done nothing wrong. It had been Katie's fault. All the guys agreed. Sometimes you had to put a woman in her place. Bruce stayed 'til closing.

When he got home after 1 a.m., all the baby's things were gone, and most of Katie's were too. He tried her cell phone, and it went straight to voicemail. He called over and over and over. Katie had taken Becky to a friend's house. She had turned the volume down on her phone, but every time he called, the screen lit up the room. Finally, at 3 a.m., she picked up, whispering so as not to wake Becky.

"What do you want, Bruce?"

"Where is Becky? Where did you take Becky?" he bellowed.

"You hit me, Bruce. It isn't fucking okay. Go sleep it off. I'll talk to you tomorrow." She ended the call and turned off her phone entirely.

Bruce sat on the floor. The room spun. He recalled Katie setting the baby down before he came after her. He saw himself putting his hand on Katie's throat. She'd just wanted a puppy for Becky. She hadn't deserved to be hit. He started to sob. *Oh, Becky, what have I done?*

By the next day, however, all remorse was forgotten. Bruce woke up, looked around, and thought, *Game on, bitch. Fuck you, Katie. How dare you?*

The first thing Bruce did after the divorce was get Becky a puppy.

In the bathroom mirror Becky stared at her reflection. Her big dark eyes, searching. Both her little brothers were blond like Katie.

"Did you find it easy to leave me because I didn't look like you?" she asked into the void.

Becky called the dogs into her room, and onto her bed. Wrapping her arms around Beretta, she buried her face into his neck and sobbed. Magnum and Ruger lay at the foot of her bed. Eventually, she fell asleep.

At 5:30 p.m., Becky woke to the sound of Bruce's truck pulling into their gravel driveway. She went into the bathroom and put a cool cloth over her eyes, then quickly washed her face. She had to get dinner going. He'd promised they'd take the dogs to Lake Woof when he got home from work.

Becky had begun looking forward to the dog park. While there was never anyone her own age there, being with Nancy and the others took her mind off being sad and made her feel less alone, though she would never admit her loneliness to anyone.

CHAPTER 11

Iris

Iris thought getting a dog might cure the loneliness *she* felt coming home to an empty apartment after working all day in her cubicle as an actuary. She also thought it might push her to be more social. After graduating from college and working for a year at an insurance company owned by a friend of the family in San Diego, she moved across the country for her new job in South Carolina. Haberland City was touted as "the new Silicon Valley" for young professionals by city planners and "best places to live" websites. In the two years since, she had not made a single friend. People thought she was odd.

She loved music and walked through the world hearing harmonies in her mind. She viscerally felt the heartbeat of the city. She loved the sound of old buildings with old pipes and picked out rhythms wherever she went. Birdsong, the beeping sound of a truck backing up, all these delighted her, like a box of auditory chocolates, but loud, sudden, unexpected noises were her nemesis. A random sneeze from a stranger at the grocery store could bring her to her knees, making her cover her ears and cry.

As difficult as it could be sometimes, the inner workings of her brain brought Iris great delight, and she sometimes became so absorbed in the cacophony of the world, joy would overtake her body, causing her right arm to extend in an ecstatic tic which looked as if she were conducting an orchestra. At times like this, she might find herself eight blocks past where she was supposed to turn, in another part of the city, before realizing she'd lost track of normal "reality." In moments she allowed herself to fully *be* herself, she experienced a bliss most people would likely never taste. The downside was a terrible sense of time and direction, and an acute sense of isolation from typical people.

Iris was a "nerd," but even nerds had a hierarchy, and she didn't seem to fit in anywhere. Though she loved music, the band nerds in high school did not appreciate when she'd go off in a different direction, the one she heard in her mind. She wasn't one for science fiction, so the Star Trek nerds were out. She wasn't competitive by nature and found chess nerds too cutthroat.

She secretly still loved Barbies, and a graphic novel series called *Baby Mouse* she'd become obsessed with as an adolescent and never let go of. Her favorite color was pink. Now still, at 25, her bed was covered with stuffed animals. She loved pop culture, Hello Kitty, Lady Gaga, costume jewelry, and cats. She'd *almost* gotten a cat before deciding to adopt Buster instead. She felt terrible guilt when she sometimes found herself wishing she'd gone in that direction.

Iris had never had a boyfriend, or a girlfriend for that matter, though she longed for friends and someone to share her life with. Gender in a partner didn't matter so much to her. She just wanted to be loved and accepted. And she had so much love to give! She looked at people and saw great beauty in even the homeliest faces. She mostly avoided eye contact, because when she looked into people's eyes, she got carried away by how mesmerizing they were, each fleck of color a jewel, the eyes glistening like kaleidoscopes. She was named after the flower, but in her heart felt she was truly named after the part of the eye that held such beauty. *If only people understood how lovely they are*, she often thought. She was one to give out compliments to strangers on the street which would sometimes startle them but brought smiles to their faces.

"I like your hat!"

"I love your shirt!"

"Oh my God! Those boots are fabulous!"

Other than the adolescent graphic novels she loved, which were more of a carryover from childhood, the way chicken soup or chocolate ice cream might be for others, Iris wasn't particularly bookish, though she was good at math. She understood numbers the way she understood music, both beautiful languages.

Iris's parents were physicians who had met in medical school. Her mother was from San Diego, her father, Hawaii. Her mother was an ophthalmologist, and her father an audiologist. "Eyes and ears," they always said. Her younger brother was currently in medical school, but they never pushed Iris in that direction, knowing how vigorous and punishing it was, and that med school would eat her alive.

Her mother loved Iris dearly but constantly chastised her for having her head in the clouds.

Her father didn't see music or numbers the way Iris did but was fascinated with how she experienced the world. The way each number had a personality and a color for her. The way she picked harmonies out of thin air, even to songs she'd never heard before. Though he was ears, and his wife was eyes, he knew neither of them saw or heard the world in the exquisite way their daughter did.

They steered her toward being an actuary, a career that would allow her to immerse herself in numbers. It would allow her to support herself, and it had been a good fit. Her family was nervous about her moving across the country by herself, but her father said, "She's got to have some adventures. She must make some mistakes. We won't be here to protect her forever."

Her family stood in a long group hug at the security checkpoint at the airport, and her mother sobbed when Iris's plane left the gate, bound for South Carolina.

Iris had been excited to be branching out on her own, but other than twice-weekly phone calls with her family, she'd had very few conversations outside of work over the last two years.

Iris lived in a dog-friendly building full of people her age, but she'd been too shy to meet any of them. She kept her head down in the elevator even though she desperately wished someone would say hello to her. Her neighbors often thought she was younger than she was, perhaps because of the Hello Kitty backpack she brought to and from work each day. Or maybe because of the pigtails she often wore in her hair. She didn't know how to do makeup and felt she looked garish whenever she tried, so she'd stopped. This only added to her youthful appearance.

This should have been an exciting time in her life. First time living away from family in a new city, in an apartment complex full of young professionals, but it was dull when you had no one to hang out with. Iris's dog Buster had not been popular in the small outdoor dog enclosure at their apartment, and she regretted not studying up on the characteristics of German shorthaired pointers before obtaining him.

She'd been considering getting a cat when her coworker mentioned in passing that his sister had a litter of puppies ready to go. When Iris was little, she did have one friend. He lived next door, and his name was Brandon, but his parents called him Buster, due to his rambunctious personality. Brandon's mom bred German shorthaired pointers. Her dogs always seemed so well behaved.

Memories of her friend who moved away when Iris was 10 flooded into her mind and heart. She remembered Brandon's mom relaxing on a big sectional, reading books, surrounded by dogs on all sides. Those dogs worshiped her.

Iris was from a cat-loving family, and had never had a dog before, but how hard could it be? Give it water and food. Love it. Take it for a walk. Get it a Hello Kitty leash? OMG, that would be awesome. The worst might be picking up poop. That's what she'd thought.

So, she called her coworker's sister, picked out the cutest of the puppies, and named him Buster. She imagined snuggling a dog when she watched TV. She imagined walking him and heaping attention on him. She had dreams of taking him to the dog enclosure attached to her apartment and of laughing with other dog owners at his cute antics. She had dreams of being *included*. Maybe Buster would attract a romantic partner into her life?

But Buster, it turned out, was not at all snuggly. It took great coaxing to get him onto the couch with her, and even if he hopped up, he stayed on the other end by her feet. He slept in a dog bed on the floor if given the choice, and at night put himself in his crate, happy to stay in the tiny dark laundry room until morning. He would wag his tail excitedly when Iris came for him in the morning, but she got the feeling he was more excited to be going outside, than to see her. Buster was obsessed with chasing squirrels up trees and then barking at them.

It had been so cute when he was a puppy. The way he stood with one paw raised and curled, completely focused. She bought him bird toys and squirrel toys and tossed them in the air for him. He would catch them, and wrestle them, and yes, kill them, pulling all the stuffing out of their insides in record time. Once, he did this to a Hello Kitty toy he stole off her bed, and it was disturbing to come home to, but Iris forgave him. After that, she remembered to shut her bedroom door, and kept him in his crate when she wasn't home.

It took only a few visits to the small dog park at the apartment for her neighbors to turn on Buster. The dog people she'd hoped to befriend began exchanging eye rolls when they saw Iris and Buster coming. No one said anything, but they kept their distance. Everyone was sick to death of listening to Buster bark up the one thin tree in the small enclosure. It was impossible to have a conversation with him there. Iris had to admit his bark was not harmonious and held no steady rhythm.

The neighbors inside the building complained about him too. As he'd grown, his bark had become loud and ferocious-sounding. Whenever anyone walked by her door or dropped off a package, he'd go nuts. She'd have to put him in his crate and cover it with a blanket, making him believe it was nighttime to get him to stop.

Now, at two years old and 60 pounds, Buster was at the vet's office for his annual checkup. Iris, avoiding eye contact with the doctor, told her about Buster's barking and that he was having a hard time fitting in.

"Perhaps you're making a big deal over nothing," the vet said. "He's healthy. He's a bird dog. It's in his genes."

"But people at the dog park in my apartment don't like it. I haven't bothered to take him there in almost a year."

The vet, smiling, said in a sing-song way, "Buster has a right to exist in this world too, you know."

The lilt of her voice caught Iris's ear, causing her to almost float off. Her arm shot out in a tic.

Iris repeated, "Buster has a right to exist in this world too," in the exact cadence the doctor had. She heard harmonies along with it, then shook her head to come back to the present moment.

The vet suggested taking him to a bigger dog park where Buster's sound would be more spread out.

"I've heard good things about Lake Woof—have you been there?"

Iris promised she would give it a try.

Buster has a right to exist in this world too.

Buster has a right to exist in this world too.

Buster has a right to exist in this world too.

An entire symphony in her head.

Iris repeated it like a mantra as she walked the oval path around the large dog section at Lake Woof. So far, Buster had never followed along with her like the other dogs followed their humans. He was content to stand at the far side of the enclosure, by the dirt mountain, barking up a tree.

Sometimes Iris imagined people in the gazebo were giving her dirty looks about his barking, and she repeated in her mind, *"Buster has a right to exist in this world too."* It calmed her. She'd walk for 30 minutes, then drag Buster away from the tree to go home. At least they both got some fresh air, and she got a little exercise, she reasoned.

One beautiful spring day, Iris was walking laps as Tommy ran up the hill to Lake Woof with Rocky. When they reached the gate at the top, Tommy punched the air with his fists and danced back and forth as he belted out the Rocky theme song, at the top of his lungs,

"Da DOM didda DOM didda DOM didda DOM," his signature entrance.

Iris loved hearing him do this, every time.

Coming through the gate, he said in a loud sportscaster voice, "And it's Buster! Buster is at the tree. Buster is determined to get that fuckin' squirrel. The squirrel taunts him, but Buster is *undeterred*. He's got nothin' but time, squirrel. One day, he's gonna catch you, and you'll regret it. Don't give up, boy! Go, Buster, go!"

Nancy and Trish and Becky were in the gazebo, and they all laughed. Iris assumed they were making fun of Buster, and her heart sank. She put her earbuds in and began walking faster. She found herself again wishing she'd gotten a cat, then felt guilty. Sometimes she dreaded the thought of dealing with Buster for the next 12 years or more. Then she'd feel even guiltier. After all, she had taken on the role of Buster's Kahu, the Hawaiian word for guardian or keeper. It was a sacred trust to be an animal's Kahu. And Buster had a right to exist in this world too.

As Iris and Buster were leaving that day, Nancy yelled, "Hey, Buster, did you get the squirrel today?"

Iris took one earbud out and turned to look at Nancy, who smiled at Buster kindly. Trish waved. Nancy tilted her head and gave Iris a double thumbs up. Even the teenager, Becky, smiled at her and Buster. Becky had *never* seemed friendly before, though Iris had recognized a certain sadness in the girl.

Iris shrugged her shoulders and grinned. "Not yet, but he's hopeful!" She decided she must have misinterpreted their laughter earlier.

"Give him time. One day you'll get it, Buster. I know you will," Nancy laughed.

"Atta boy, Buster!" Tommy yelled.

Iris smiled.

One small interaction, one moment of kindness, and she'd been buoyed. Maybe she could do this. Maybe she could be Buster's mom. Perhaps there was hope for them yet.

Iris gave Nancy and the others a grateful wave as she drove out of the parking lot, spirits lifted. She let out a long exhale. "They don't hate us, Buster." Then sang to him, "We have a right to exist in this world too."

On her way out of the park, she noticed Becky's dad's truck swerving up the winding road toward Lake Woof. He crossed the yellow lines in her direction, scaring her half to death, and she quickly veered onto the shoulder to avoid him. Iris's hand hovered over the horn, but she thought better of it and kept going toward home.

CHAPTER 12

About Liam

One slow afternoon at the dog park, Ann, Nancy, Iris, and Trish were sitting in the gazebo. Iris told them about seeing Bruce's truck swerving all over the road a couple of weeks ago. They all had similar stories about him.

"That poor kid," Nancy said, thinking of Becky. They all concurred. After they chewed on Bruce's faults for a while, Trish changed the subject and began complaining about the men where she worked. The others nodded in support.

"Gay men can be so catty," she said. "I had no idea half the salon had hit on Tyler while we were together."

Nancy shook her head, "Men," she said.

After a while, Trish asked, "What kind of work do *you* do, Ann?"

"I'm a professor at the university, and I also write books," Ann said.

Trish had been growing on Ann as the women shared small confidences in the gazebo. Ann listened to Trish's story about her doomed engagement. She witnessed Trish be kind to Iris, who was odd, but sweet. Trish also loved Choco, but then again, who didn't?

"Real books? Like, at Barnes and Noble? Like Nicholas Sparks?" Trish asked.

Ann nodded. "Yes. Well, not exactly, but yes," she chuckled. "I teach about social justice, white fragility. Mostly. I write nonfiction."

Iris closed her eyes and tilted her head, enjoying the feel of the air on her skin, and the cadence of Ann's voice.

Buster was barking up a tree on the other side of the enclosure, but far enough away not to bother them. Teddy lay in a heap at Nancy's feet. Choco had already run the fence with Wayne's dogs. He walked over and put his paws up on Trish's lap. She scooped him up and began lazily stroking him from head to toe. Gigi basked in the sun in the green space. The leaves on the trees had filled out as spring wore on, rustling in a warm almost-summer breeze.

Trish asked Ann, "Is Choco a rescue, or did you get him from a breeder?"

Ann replied, "A breeder. It had to be a purebred Dachshund for my son. There was no fighting it."

"Why?" Trish asked. "I mean, I'm not judging or anything," she said, even though she was, just a little bit.

Ann began telling them the story of Liam and Choco.

When Liam was five years old, he became obsessed with what he'd then called "hot dogs." Ann bought him a stuffed Dachshund, thinking it might appease his longing, but it only made it worse. He carried it around all day, talking to it, and slept with it every night.

Liam spoke incessantly of the day he would get a real Dachshund. Using crayons and markers, he drew hundreds of pictures of his one-day dog. He had a vision board, devoted to Dachshunds, a bulletin board in his room where he printed out photos from the Internet. He named his imaginary chocolate-colored dog Choco. Liam talked to strangers about him as if he were real. The refrigerator was covered in Choco pictures he'd made. His dinner table talk often included statements like, "When I get my real hot dog," or "I bet Choco's going to *love* hamburgers."

After almost three years of this, it was evident his obsession with chocolate-colored Dachshunds was not going away.

Liam had been an even-tempered, easy baby. He was inquisitive, but not demanding, as a toddler. While other kids shoved their way into toy rooms at daycare, he waited patiently for his turn. He got along with everyone, was no outcast, but was also content to play by himself. When Liam was six, he would stand at his Lego table building with bricks, as the stuffed Dachshund sat at his feet. At seven, he read the entire first Harry Potter book out loud to the stuffed Dachshund tucked under his arm.

He didn't beg for a dog, merely prepared for Choco's inevitable arrival. Liam knew Choco would eventually come; that's just how it was.

As they approached his eighth birthday, Ann finally gave in. One night after she'd tucked him into bed, she got onto a Dachshund breeder website and saw Choco for the first time. It was a headshot of a bleary-eyed baby. His eyes were watery as if he'd just been pulled from a sleeping puppy pile and startled by the flash of a camera. His fur was dark brown with caramel-colored markings. His eyes looked like black marbles. The puppy was so small, so vulnerable, almost pathetic really. His ears appeared too big for his body. In that moment, all Liam's drawings, all the Choco talk, all the love she had for her son, and all the love Liam had for Choco collided, propelling her fingers to type the breeder a message.

"Is this puppy available? And if so, when will he be ready for adoption?"

The breeder emailed back 15 minutes later—yes. The puppy would be ready the day before Liam's eighth birthday.

Was it kismet?

Ann went to pick up the puppy by herself. Choco was just as cute as he'd appeared in the picture. He was just as pathetic as he'd looked as well, and he cried all the way home in a box on the front seat of the Volvo. She set him down in the living room, and he peed on her gleaming hardwood floors and cried some more, no doubt wondering where his mother was. Ann picked him up and comforted him. Choco snuggled right onto her chest and under her chin.

Soon the carpool mom dropped off Liam in their driveway, and as he made his way up the front steps, Ann placed the puppy back into the cardboard box she'd brought Choco home in.

Liam entered and called out, "Hi, Mom!" He dropped his backpack on the floor and raced over to give her a hug.

Ann could not remember ever feeling this giddy about anything in her life. Gob smacked and scared were the emotions she felt when she found out she was expecting Liam. But this moment of anticipation was unconflicted pure joy.

Ann reached out and held Liam's hands. Looking him in the eye, she said, "Sweetie, I have an early birthday present for you."

Liam smiled, as she gestured toward the box, imagining what Lego she might have gotten him.

When he pulled back the flaps of the box, Liam sucked in his breath. His mouth opened, but no words came out. He froze.

Goosebumps covered his arms and legs and went right up over the crown of his head. He knew Choco would come one day but had not expected it *that* day. He gently picked up the puppy and held him to his chest.

"Hi, Buddy! You made it! Hi, Choco!" he whispered, his voice catching in his throat, tears in his eyes. It felt otherworldly, more a reuniting than an introduction. With all his heart, Liam felt his brother had finally arrived.

Ann had always marked the day as one of the happiest of her life, watching her son's dream come true.

Anticipating long days at school and work, they'd tried to crate-train Choco, but he was inconsolable. After two nights of hell with Choco howling and pooping all over his crate and vomiting in distress, they moved him to Liam's bed, and that's where he slept happy and cozy every night until the day Liam left for college. Liam placed his stuffed animal Choco placeholder on his dresser, and that was where it stayed.

Liam attended Hopewell, a small private K-12 school close to the college. Dropping him off that first day, Ann pulled his teacher aside. "If he's distracted, it's because he got a puppy over the weekend."

Ms. Julie's mouth opened wide, and her eyes went bright. Her hands went to her heart. "He got Choco?"

Everyone at Hopewell knew about Liam's imaginary dog.

"Yes, but I'm a little worried about him. We left Choco in the bathroom because he couldn't handle the crate. I'm afraid he'll howl all day," Ann added, "Liam was inconsolable this morning having to leave him. I almost couldn't get him to come to school—he was so worried about the puppy."

"Why not bring him?" Julie asked. "The kids would love to have a puppy in class!" And that was how Choco ended up at school, where he would go every day, right up through Liam's high school years. By the time Liam was in sixth grade, the children took a vote and officially made Choco the school mascot, and a Dachshund statue was placed in the garden. Before the ceremonial unveiling of the statue, Liam read a poem. Earlier in the year, Ms. Julie had given the class an assignment to write about themselves using the poem "Where I'm From" by George Ella Lyon as a prompt. Instead of writing about himself, Liam had written his poem about Choco. The children laughed delightedly when the first thing Choco did was walk over, lift his leg, and pee on the likeness of himself.

For years, Liam held the imaginary Choco in his mind and heart, but now the real Choco sat at his feet while he built with Legos. The real Choco ran around the playground during recess. The real Choco was there when he learned algebra and American history. When he wasn't on someone's lap, Choco slept on his cushion at the front of Liam's classrooms beside the teachers. He'd served as an unofficial emotional support animal for the entire school for students and faculty alike. And then it was time for Liam to go to college.

Though Ann joked it would be a burden to care for Choco after Liam left for school, she secretly liked the idea. Having him there would make the house feel less empty.

Ann stopped talking for a moment. Her attention drifted to a conversation she regretted.

Liam hadn't wanted to come home for Thanksgiving break his first year. In a phone call, he said he wanted to stay at school in Florida and surf with some of his new friends. He said he'd always wanted to learn to surf.

Ann had folded her arms over her chest, raising her eyebrows.

"Since when? This is news to me," she said curtly into the phone.

Ann reminded him he'd already promised to come home for Thanksgiving, and when you made a promise, you kept your word. Really, she just missed him so much.

Nancy interrupted Ann's thoughts.

"Your son should be home from school soon for summer, right? You gotta bring him by. We'd all love to meet him," she laughed, "Choco's brother," she added, smiling broadly.

Ann looked down at her lap. She bit her lip, pressed her palms into her thighs, and leaned forward. She felt nauseous. While she'd told them about Liam in bits and pieces, and shared more today, she'd not told them the big thing. She closed her eyes and took a couple of long slow breaths.

Nancy said, "Ann, are you okay?"

Ann glanced up and saw Iris looking at her, with her brow furrowed in worry. Ann looked sideways at Nancy, then back to Trish and Choco. She turned toward Nancy again and took a breath.

Her throat tightened, and she swallowed hard. Her voice came out high-pitched, smaller than normal.

"I always thought of the day we got Choco... as one of the happiest of my life. It was certainly the happiest day of Liam's... but now when I think of it, it's painful. I want to turn back the clock. My son died five months ago. He was hit by a drunk driver when he was home for Thanksgiving break. It happened right in front of the Butterfly Garden Café."

Nancy sucked in her breath, and her hands flew to her heart. "Oh my God, Ann, I had no idea. I'm so sorry!" She moved over on the bench and wrapped her arms around her friend. Nancy briefly remembered hearing about the accident, involving a drunk driver in a Mack truck, killing a teenage boy. The Butterfly Café was an iconic Haberland City landmark, and it closed for a week after the accident because the staff, most of them teenagers, were so traumatized by it.

Ann said, "He didn't want to come home for his school break." Her voice caught. "He wanted to stay in Florida with his friends, but I pushed the issue. It's all my fault. If I hadn't insisted he come home, he'd be alive."

Ann began to sob. She finally said out loud what she'd been thinking for months. It was *her* fault Liam had died. She'd been beating herself up relentlessly since the accident. Trish put Choco down and came to Ann's other side. She wrapped her arms around Ann and Nancy both, hoping to absorb some of Ann's pain. Iris stood up, hovering around them, not knowing what to do. Tears filled her eyes. She searched through her Hello Kitty backpack, found a pack of tissues, and handed them to Ann.

When Ann's sobbing eased up, the women sat in silence for a while. The leaves continued rustling on that beautiful blue-sky day.

Nancy finally said, "You know, Ann, that kind of thinking will do you no good. You could just as easily have let him stay in Florida, and something bad could have happened to him surfing. Parents make their kids come home during break. They usually don't die. It was a terrible, terrible fluke, but it isn't your fault."

Ann looked at her feet and nodded. Logically, she knew that was true.

Trish added earnestly, "I know someone who is a medium if you ever want to do a reading. She connects with people who have passed."

Ann fought the urge to roll her eyes, but, knowing Trish meant well, simply said, "I'll think about that."

Finally, Iris said tentatively, "Tell us more about Liam, Ann. If you want to."

Ann pulled a tissue out of the packet Iris had given her, blew her nose, and began to talk.

When Liam had gone off to college, Ann found herself crying as she did the dishes. She hadn't expected to be hit with empty nest grief and felt a bit ridiculous. It wasn't as if he'd gone off to war. He was living in a cushy dorm room. She'd set it up for him herself with new pillows, sheets, and towels.

Ann had experienced grief in losing each of her parents, but Liam's *death* left her reeling on a whole different level. She felt pain physically in every cell of her body. Ann felt robbed of time with Liam. She felt angry. She hated the man in the truck who had killed him. Driving past the site of the accident was unavoidable. Ann had to pull over on the side of the road more than once. Hands over her face, she'd screamed until her throat was raw.

Aside from making Liam come home for break, Ann had so many other regrets. She'd never taken him to Europe. She'd never taken him to Disney. What kid hadn't been to Disney? Ann regretted all those times she happily ignored him, reading a book while he was absorbed in Lego or video games. How many times had she tuned out his constant chatter when he was little? What had been more important than listening to him? Why had she not been more present? Sometimes Ann felt a physical pain in her chest when she thought about the fact that he would never fall in love. He'd never get the opportunity to have children.

Liam had been a social kid with a strong friend group. He was kind to everyone and possessed a certain indefinable coolness like his father. He was strikingly handsome, too, like his father. Ann regretted not telling him about his father.

Ann had met Liam's father on a yoga retreat in Costa Rica. They'd locked eyes the first night and subsequently spent four nights in his cabana. They had not exchanged contact information when they parted. She'd never felt sexier or more alive than the time she'd spent with Ben. She barely knew him, but remembered him saying he had never wanted children, so she never tried to find him. Yes, there had been a moment when a condom had slipped off inside of her, but she hadn't really worried about it at the time. What were the odds?

A month after the retreat, she felt sweaty and nauseous while giving a lecture. She made it through the hour but soon found herself slumped over the sink in the faculty bathroom. She thought it was the flu, but by the end of the day, it'd passed. It happened twice more before she remembered the flu didn't wax and wane.

Ann stood in her bathroom that evening, staring at two pink lines. How many times had she judged students who had accidentally gotten pregnant and had to drop out? She'd always thought of them as careless or reckless. And now here she was.

Just behind the initial fear was a hint, a wiggle, a spark of pure joy that surprised her. It was as if she and this soul were already in cahoots.

She believed in bodily autonomy and a woman's right to choose. She made a rational pros-and-cons list, but her heart never considered terminating the pregnancy. Not for a moment.

To appear competent, Ann told her administration she'd planned this. She said she used a sperm donor and would be raising the baby on her own. Ann would be using the college's stellar daycare. These matters were private, and that's all they needed to know. Independent, feminist, modern woman, check. Her colleagues applauded her decision. They threw her a baby shower a month before Liam was born. Her best friend Helen held her hand as she pushed, bringing Liam earthside.

That night, moonlight poured in through the hospital window as Ann gazed at her newborn son who stared right back into her eyes. She thought, "*Here* is the love of my life." Ann named him after her father, who had died of a heart attack when she was 29, just a year before Liam was born.

Ann grew up in Haberland City. In the early '70s, when she was in first grade, a black family moved in next door with a little girl named Helen who was Ann's age. Helen's family was the first to integrate their upper middle-class neighborhood. Ann's dad was the first to go over and introduce himself. Ann and Helen bonded instantly and had been lifelong best friends.

Not long after Helen's family moved in, a brick went through their window. After that, Ann's dad accompanied Ann and Helen on their walk to school every single day for the next three years to make sure they were safe.

When Ann was 10 years old, her father took her to an old city park and showed her the abandoned foundation of a swimming pool.

"When we integrated, the city filled in the pool rather than have their white children swim with black children."

Ann became outraged. This started a fire for social justice in her that continued throughout her life and into her career. After a devastating act of police brutality almost killed one of the students at her college, she was asked by the Black Student Union to become one of the liaisons between students and police. She was part of a program called Building Bridges, which helped educate the police about racial discrimination. Somehow, perhaps the result of her years of meditation practice, Ann was able to stay calm when white police officers became defensive and shut down. She could get past their armor and gently make them aware of their blind spots. Building Bridges had been recognized locally and nationally. Ann was proud to be a small part of it.

Ann's mother passed away 10 years ago after a long battle with Alzheimer's, the last five years of which she had no recognition of Ann, or of Liam.

Before Liam was born, Ann thought she would never have kids and was at peace with it. After he arrived, she couldn't imagine life without him.

The nurses fawned over Liam. "All that blond hair!"

"He must look like his father."

Ann smiled, remembering Ben. Grateful.

When he was four years old, Liam asked why he didn't have a daddy, and Ann told him there were all kinds of families. Some had a mommy and a daddy. Some had two mommies. Some had just one mommy. Some had two daddies. Some had just one daddy. "You get what you get, and every family is different." Liam seemed satisfied with her answer.

Ann was grateful for her fulfilling career. She loved teaching and knew she was lucky having on-site daycare and a part-time nanny to fill in the gaps. It was a privilege most American women did not have, but sometimes it was hard being the sole parent to absorb worries or concerns about Liam.

When he was a teen, he'd roll his eyes at her questions about his comings and goings, and she would remind him, "You are the most important thing in the world to me. I hope you can appreciate that. I am only ever trying to do what is best for you. I am trying to keep you safe."

Liam's tone would lose its edge.

"Okay, Mom," he would sigh. "What can I do to make you feel safe?"

"Text me the second you get there. Listen to your inner guidance. If anything seems off, you leave a situation, okay? I will come get you, no questions asked."

Liam would agree, and Ann would let him go. Over and over, she let him go, giving him as much freedom as she could stand.

Now Liam was dead, and what had any of it mattered?

Ann felt as if she were constantly searching for him and couldn't find him anywhere.

Five months in, the idea of getting dressed and taking Choco to the dog park still sometimes felt insurmountable. She was having trouble sleeping. Ann had always been in control of her life, but now she was lost. She dreamt she was in charge of someone's baby and had forgotten to feed it. She'd forgotten where she left it. Desperately searching for the baby, deeply ashamed of failing at her responsibility, she feared the baby had died.

Waking up was no relief.

Every new day, Ann had to convince her brain it was true. Liam was really gone. Every new day, she beat herself up for making him come home for Thanksgiving break.

The women sat in silence, absorbing Ann's words. After a while, Ann looked at Iris, swallowed, and said softly, "Thanks for asking about him, Iris. He was the best kid. Honestly, he really was."

Iris closed her eyes as if listening to something far away, then sang, in an angelic tone, "Honestly, he really was."

She opened her eyes, looked directly at Ann and continued, "And his beautiful mother *misses* him."

They held each other's gaze as love and empathy poured into Ann. Eye contact with Iris felt somehow healing. After a long moment, Ann said, "Thank you, Iris, I do."

That night, Ann looked at the photo of Liam and Choco on her bedside table as she always did before turning out the light. She realized it had done her soul good to talk about Liam out loud. To have others witness and validate her pain, and to *know* Liam somehow. Ann fell into a sound sleep and woke up refreshed for the first time in months.

CHAPTER 13

Gun Talk

That day, Ed and his dog Henry entered the enclosure and headed toward the gazebo. As he got closer, Ed realized Choco's owner Ann was crying. Trish, Nancy, and Iris were comforting her. Nancy looked up and waved Ed away, which was fine with Ed. He hoped Ann was okay, but *strong feelings* were not his specialty. He walked over and leaned against the fence, waiting for Tommy and Rocky to arrive.

When they did, Ed shushed Tommy when he began singing the Rocky theme song at the top of his lungs.

"Ann's upset," he said. Tommy glanced toward the women in the gazebo, a look of concern on his face.

"Don't know what about," Ed added, before Tommy could ask.

They walked a few laps together and then noticed Bruce coming into the dog park with the two older huskies. Becky followed several steps behind with the third dog.

Meeting them at the gate, Tommy said, "Hey, something's up with Ann, but we don't know what it is. Nancy said they needed privacy."

Bruce looked at the gazebo, assessed the situation, and nodded, then said, "That's fine. Becky and I won't intrude."

The dogs took off to play. Becky put her earbuds in and began walking laps.

Ed, Tommy, and Bruce leaned against the fence.

"Beautiful dogs," Ed said to Bruce.

Bruce said, "Thank you."

Tommy asked, "What are their names?"

Bruce replied, "Beretta, Magnum, and Ruger."

Ed raised his eyebrows. "I take it you're a gun enthusiast?"

Bruce sized Ed up. "You got me," he replied.

"What about you?" Bruce asked.

Ed said, "Lifelong member of the NRA. After I got out of the military, I used to hunt deer with some buddies. Now, I only do target practice, sometimes some skeet shooting."

Bruce nodded approvingly, turned his attention to Tommy. "And you?"

"No. I've never held a gun in my life," Tommy replied.

Both men looked at Tommy, considering this.

Bruce said, "And you grew up right here in South Carolina?"

Tommy nodded. "Born and bred!" Then he added, "Single mom." He continued, "They started those active shooter drills when I was in high school. It was freaking scary. I guess it kind of traumatized me. I want nothing to do with guns."

Bruce said, "But that's why we *need* guns. To protect ourselves from things like that. We should be arming all the teachers."

Ed interjected, "Actually that doesn't work. You can't expect a civilian under severe stress to be accurate. Even trained soldiers often miss the mark. Guns in schools would be a very dangerous situation. Imagine a teacher accidentally kills a student?"

Bruce looked at Ed, incredulously.

Tommy said, "I just think we need common-sense gun laws."

With a condescending sneer, Bruce replied, "Tommy, the problem with that idea is bad guys aren't following the laws. Bad guys aren't purchasing guns legally. The only thing to stop a bad guy with a gun is a good guy with a gun."

Bruce had purchased his own gun illegally but failed to see the irony of his statement.

Ed said, "I'm not opposed to *some* gun laws. When I was in the military, I couldn't run around willy-nilly with my gun. There were rules. It had to be locked up when not in use. And civilians certainly don't need automatic weapons."

"That's what I'm saying," said Tommy. "You need a license to drive a car. You need a background check for most jobs. Why shouldn't we need some regulations on buying weapons that can kill? Like, the whole reason for a gun is to kill something or someone."

Bruce's body tensed, with the energy of a rattlesnake about to strike. "I have a Second Amendment right to have whatever kind of gun I want. As many as I want. The day they come for my guns is the day they'll regret it. I'll tell you what—they'll take my guns over my dead body."

Bruce made it sound as if he had a full arsenal at home, when in reality it was just the one handgun in his bedside table drawer.

Ed said, "Trust me. If there comes a day when the government wants your guns, there'll be little you can do about it."

Bruce said, "We'll see about that," folding his arms tightly over his chest.

Becky rounded the corner, and Bruce called her over,

"Now, my daughter Becky here appreciates guns. Tell 'em what you know about guns, Becks."

Tommy and Ed looked at Becky.

She paused, staring back at them. Then, shrugging her shoulders, she turned to meet Bruce's eye.

"I know I'm a damned good shot," she deadpanned, staring him down.

"Whoa," Tommy said. "Don't mess with Becky!"

She held Bruce's gaze for another moment, then put her earbuds back in and continued her laps.

Tommy and Ed chuckled.

Bruce did not laugh. They'd only been at Lake Woof for 20 minutes, but he called for Becky and the dogs, saying it was time to go home.

CHAPTER 14

Braiding and Ogling

Bruce's truck swerved up the hill, chugging loudly into the parking lot, late one afternoon. Nancy shook her head. "I don't get it. Why does anyone need to be so dang big and noisy? Seems like he's overcompensating for something." She winked. Iris and Trish chuckled.

Bruce got out of the truck and lowered the tailgate. The two older huskies leapt out onto the pavement. The younger dog pulled Becky, per usual, as they walked toward the gate. Once inside, the three dogs tended to stay together, often singling out another dog to chase or intimidate like a pack of menacing teenagers. They entered the dog park, and Becky joined Nancy, Trish, and Iris in the gazebo. Gretchen was patrolling Lake Woof, bossing people around and blowing her whistle. Bruce was leaning against the fence, scrolling on his phone and looked up as she passed him on a lap around the walking path. He looked at her critically, noting the crappy job she'd done on her braids. Did the woman have no pride? Loose ends all over the place. She even missed a chunk in the back. He could do better.

When Bruce first got custody of Becky, her hair was always a mess. He hadn't even noticed, until Becky told him another girl made fun of her at school over it. The next day, he tried to put her hair in a ponytail, but it took him forever, and it was a disaster. Becky cried and ripped it out. He'd been livid, but knew she was right. He'd done a terrible job.

He fretted about this, knowing Katie would do better. She used things like this to try to make him reconsider their custody arrangement. "She needs her mother," Katie would say at hand-off. "There is a lot about being a girl you can't help her with, Bruce."

"Bullshit!" he'd reply. "No way, Katie."

The next time Becky was at Katie's, he spent hours studying braiding on YouTube. He started by tying three strings together and progressed to working on a mop. Then, he went to Walmart and bought a full-sized Barbie head to practice on. No way was he going to let Katie give him shit about Becky's hair. He worked on ponytails too, perfecting his technique, making them neat and using a curling iron to give them some flair.

Within weeks, he could braid better than any other mother at the school. He worked on French braids, reverse French braids, all types. Becky's teachers and the girls in her class would "ooh" and "ahh" each day over Bruce's creations. Becky loved the attention the first two years, and Bruce did too. Being able to braid his daughter's hair got him laid more than once by single moms at Becky's school (and one married one). They didn't suspect a man who would braid his daughter's hair to also be a jerk. But the mommies weren't 19-year-old cheerleaders, and it didn't take long for them to figure out something wasn't quite right with him. More than one thought his obsession with his daughter was a little creepy.

As much as he loved sending Becky to school with elaborate braids, he loved sending her to Katie's with them even more and would make sure those Friday braids every other weekend were spectacular. Becky would hop into Katie's car with her backpack, and the second they rounded the corner out of Bruce's sight, she'd begin dismantling his handiwork. Becky did it instinctively, protecting Katie from the braids' gloating before her mother even got a chance to take a good look at them.

By fourth grade, Becky got tired of having her hair yanked and pulled every morning before school. Bruce forced the braiding sessions a few more months but finally got sick of her complaining, and they gave it up. He felt it was another example of how ungrateful children could be.

Bruce took one more derisive look at Gretchen, then went back to scrolling on his phone while the dogs ran about.

Lately, banter in the gazebo came to a halt, and people began watching their own dogs more cautiously whenever the huskies arrived.

This day, Ruger charged toward Gigi. Tucking his nose under her, he flipped her onto her back. She lay there belly up as Ruger snarled at her, hackles raised. Magnum and Beretta circled around her.

Trish got up and yelled to Bruce, "Hey, can you call your dogs? They're being aggressive with Gigi."

Before Bruce could react, Becky ran over and yelled, "Ruger! Knock it off!" Ruger let Gigi go and came running toward Becky. Beretta and Magnum followed.

"Quit being bullies," Becky chastised her dogs. They ran off toward the other end of the park.

Swaggering over, Bruce said to Trish, "You might want to lighten up. They were just playing. That's what dogs do."

"It didn't look like play to me," Trish replied, a tight smile trying to disguise her anger, for Becky's sake.

"Well maybe you don't know their language. You're not a dog," he said, running his eyes from her head down to her Reebok sneakers, then back up her leggings, her midriff, and landing squarely on her chest. "Far from it," he added, raising his eyebrows lasciviously.

"Ew, Dad. Don't be disgusting," Becky said. She looked at Trish apologetically. He was such an embarrassment when he'd had a few drinks. He'd stopped at Malone's Tavern after work.

Trish gave Bruce a dirty look as she called for Gigi. She snapped Gigi's leash to her collar and started heading toward the gate. Looking over her shoulder, she glared at Bruce as she made her way out of the enclosure, muttering under her breath, "Freaking pig."

He laughed, "I guess *someone's* on the rag?"

Iris scowled at him.

Nancy said, "Bruce, that isn't called for."

He staggered toward Nancy and bowed down dramatically before her.

"So sorry, ma'am, for my *uncouthness*," he said, dripping with sarcasm.

Nancy sat with her arms crossed, looking straight at him. No smile.

Becky folded in on herself, wanting to die of embarrassment.

Bruce said, "Well, I can see someone as low class as myself isn't welcome here, so I'm just gonna take off for a bit. Becky, watch the dogs. I'll pick you up later."

Bruce had gotten into the habit of dropping Becky and the huskies off at the dog park, saying he had things he needed to get done, groceries, and other errands. The truth was he felt out of place there. While everyone gathered to talk, he held awkward silence, and when he did speak, he usually said something that offended at least one or two people. And there was always some *whiny bitch* wanting to complain about Ruger. Better to personally avoid the park as much as possible, though he conceded the pup needed the exercise.

CHAPTER 15

Shane

Bruce dropped Becky off at the dog park once again to manage the dogs on her own. None of the people she usually talked to were there, so Becky began walking laps, listening to Nirvana, one earbud in. The other bud was broken, and she let it dangle down by her left hip. Becky noticed Zen Guy sitting in the usual spot on the far end of the park, his little Australian cattle dog under the bench by his feet.

She'd seen the guy before. His nose always in a book, he never came into the gazebo to talk to the others. Zen Guy wore expensive-looking linen pants, and V-neck T-shirts that didn't look like the cheap shirts Bruce bought in bulk at Walmart. Zen Guy's shirts were more fitted. He looked like he was in good shape for an old guy. Becky figured he must be at least 40, maybe older. He reminded her of Sting, and she rolled her eyes, thinking, *He probably does* yoga. She'd seen him pull into the park in a Lexus. Becky watched him through her long dark bangs and wondered if he was some type of doctor. Maybe a psychologist? She knew the type. Bruce was pressured by the school to have her see a shrink for a while last year, but she'd refused to talk, and it didn't last long.

Zen Guy's dog's name was Blue. He was a short dog, and speckled, and cute in his own way. Blue didn't let humans pet him. He didn't bite or anything, but he dodged away when she reached down to let him sniff her hand a couple of different times. He liked to lie on his belly by Zen Guy's feet. She'd seen Blue put Ruger in his place a few times, and it had always needed doing.

Zen Guy had never given Becky the time of day.

Rounding the path, Becky saw her dogs barreling toward a petite labradoodle who had been walking with a retired couple that always arrived dressed in matching L.L. Bean clothes.

Damn it, Ruger, she thought. *It's the second dog he's gone after today.*

Suddenly, Blue bolted across the green space toward the labradoodle, cutting the huskies off. The huskies pivoted and ran in another direction.

The labradoodle's owners were furious. Pointing at Blue, the woman said, "That's the second time he's charged at Mitsy!" Blue looped around and positioned himself back at Zen Guy's feet.

The woman hooked Mitsy to her leash and handed the dog off to her husband. She marched across the park to Zen Guy. "Your dog just tried to attack our dog."

Zen Guy looked up from his book, studying her. "I don't think so. My dog isn't aggressive. He's a cattle dog. He herds other dogs. That's what they do."

The woman bristled. "I don't see any other dogs just lying in wait to prey on our Mitsy!"

Zen Guy slowly shook his head, shrugged, and went back to his book.

"Your dog is a terrorist!" the woman said over her shoulder, walking back toward her husband and dog. They hustled toward the gate in a huff.

Becky, walking past Zen Guy, rolled her eyes and shrugged. Noting her sympathetic face, he said, "Blue's a cattle dog. They aren't aggressive. Heelers like order."

He folded his book and set it down beside him. "My name is Shane," he said, holding out his hand for her to shake.

Becky looked at his hand like it might have cooties, reluctantly reaching out her own to let him shake it.

"I'm Becky," she answered, then apologetically said, "My dad's the asshole with the huskies."

Shane smiled, knowing immediately who she was referring to. He'd seen Bruce at the park. His truck was hard to miss. Shane gestured toward the open space on the bench beside him. Becky tentatively sat down. Shane wanted to protect Blue's reputation at the dog park, so he began telling Becky about him.

Shane had been living in an apartment complex close to the university. Blue had belonged to a frat house across the street. Shane walked by him every day on his way to work (and Becky had been right; he was a shrink). The frat boys neglected Blue. They left him outside all day in a small fenced front yard. His water bowl seemed to always be empty, even on hot days. There was no place for him to take shelter from the sun. Shane would often pour bottled water over the fence into his metal bowl.

On weekends, Shane would sometimes walk by and see the frat boys teasing the dog. They'd play toss, throwing toys over his head, making him run back and forth, but never giving him the satisfaction of allowing him to catch one.

"Speak! Speak!" they commanded the dog, but Blue just sat there, tilting his head, hopefully.

"This dog is so stupid!" he once heard one of them say, and Shane felt a protective anger rise in him. Odd, because he wasn't really an animal person. He liked to travel, and pets didn't fit his lifestyle.

He noticed the dog getting thinner and thinner. He began bringing him dog biscuits, slipping a few through the fence each time he walked by. The little cattle dog inhaled the treats, and soon wagged his tail like crazy every time he saw Shane coming. Shane started petting him through the fence, giving him scratches behind his ears. Sometimes various frat boys would notice Shane giving the dog affection through the fence, but they never said anything to him about it. It seemed no one really cared about the dog. This went on for several months, and then one day, he was gone. His empty water bowl sat overturned in the yard.

At this point in Shane's story, Choco came by and put his paws on Shane's lap. Blue was unthreatened. He didn't budge.

"Who's this?" Shane asked, charmed by the little dog with the long body and long ears.

"That's Ann's dog Choco. He wants you to pick him up." Becky pointed toward the gazebo where Ann and Nancy and Iris were chatting. "She's a college professor."

"Really?" Shane asked, lifting Choco onto his lap.

Becky said, "She's the lady in the green shirt. Nancy calls Choco the Mayor of Lake Woof, because he likes to greet everyone personally, humans and dogs alike."

Shane nodded and smiled at Choco, who looked up at him with his dark soulful eyes. "He's kind of little for the big dog section, isn't he?"

Becky said, "Yeah, but Ann and Nancy like to sit in the gazebo and talk, and he gets along fine with the big dogs, so it's whatever."

She continued, "So where was Blue? You obviously found him."

Shane let Choco hop back down and continued his story.

He explained that he waited a few days, and then one morning on his way to work, he marched up the front steps and knocked on the frat house door. The stench of stale beer hit him as the door opened, and a disheveled young man, still half asleep, finally answered. "Dude, it's eight in the morning."

Shane asked, "What happened to the dog?"

The frat boy scratched his head and said, "Yeah, *technically*, we weren't supposed to have dogs here, and someone ratted us out. We figured it was you. Was it?"

Shane said, "No! I loved that dog," surprising himself. He *loved* that dog?

The frat boy said, "Okay, whatever, but we had to get rid of it. I think Ryan took it to a shelter." The young man rubbed his eyes and yawned.

"Dude, I gotta go back to bed," he said, slowly shutting the door in Shane's face.

Shane, who never wanted a dog, found himself calling three different animal shelters to see if they had recently taken in a cattle dog. Each one said no.

That night attempting to sleep, all he could think about was the little dog. Where was he? Was he hungry? What if they hadn't

MICHELLE O'NEIL

taken him to a shelter but just dropped him on the side of a road somewhere? Shane couldn't bear the thought.

That weekend, he decided to look in person. There were four shelters in the city, and he would go to each one, just in case.

Walking down the rows of cages was heartbreaking. There were so many terrified and miserable dogs. Strays. Mamas with puppies. Elderly dogs. The volunteer explained how some of the older dogs got turned in when their families could no longer take care of their vet bills. Other dogs were surrendered when their owners died. As he walked down the aisles, some dogs trembled. Some howled. Some barked angrily, showing their teeth. Others had given up, not even lifting their heads as he passed the cages. It felt like they were in prison. He considered taking one of these dogs—they were so pathetic—but reminded himself he didn't want a dog. He was just looking for his buddy. Just in case he was there. Row after row, he searched.

At the final shelter, in the last cage of the last row, he saw a dog with similar markings. The dog's back was to the cage door, and he was curled into a tight ball, cowering. This dog looked too small to be his little friend; it couldn't be him.

Shane called to him, "Hey, little guy."

The dog ignored him.

Shane called to him again. "Hey, buddy?" The dog tipped his head.

Could it be?

The dog slowly lifted his nose into the air, catching Shane's scent. Suddenly, he leapt up and ran to the cage door, crying pathetically. He'd found him!

Becky said, "Oh my God. It's like his spirit called out to you and told you to keep looking for him!"

"Exactly!" Shane said. He'd never put it that way, but that's precisely what it had felt like.

"He's a *good* dog," he told Becky, wanting to erase the woman's assessment of Blue as a "terrorist" from her mind.

"I can see that," Becky said. "I've never had a problem with him."

She paused, then said, "Rich people are assholes," referring to the woman who had been so up in arms about Blue.

Shane laughed. "Hey, I grew up without a lot of money, but now I have a good career and make some. I think having money only amplifies what you already are. If you are generous, it allows you to be even more so, and if you are inclined to be an asshole, money makes you a bigger one."

Becky paused, considering what he'd said.

Just then, they heard Bruce's truck. They watched as he pulled into the parking lot.

"Then I guess it's good my dad doesn't have a pot to piss in," she said, getting up to leave.

"Nice talking to you," she added.

"It was very nice to meet you, Becky," Shane said. "Thanks for listening."

Walking toward the gate, she called the huskies over. She got Ruger leashed up, and they headed out of the enclosure. Bruce got out of the truck to help the two bigger dogs up into the back, and the younger one got in the front with Becky.

Shane watched them drive away. He wondered if the man might be drunk, noting the truck weaving back and forth across the yellow lines. He hoped not. Becky seemed like a good kid. *She must take after her mother*, he thought, before putting his nose back into his book.

After that, Shane tried to be more social at the dog park. Partly because he wanted to protect Blue's reputation, and partly because he'd been charmed by Becky. Instead of keeping to himself on the bench at the far end of the enclosure, he now made a point to sit in the gazebo and engage in light conversation most days.

"Tell them about how you got Blue," Becky said a few weeks later. "It's a cool story!" she added.

Nancy, Iris, Trish, and Tommy were there that day and sat riveted by Shane's tale.

"Funny how the right dog always comes to us, isn't it?" Nancy said, smiling at Blue.

"Funny how the right dog always comes to us, isn't it?" Iris parroted, before glancing at Buster on the other side of the green space. Per usual, he was barking up a tree. She suddenly looked as if she might cry, and said, "We have to go."

They watched Iris leave the dog park abruptly with Buster, shoulders hunched forward. She didn't wave her usual goodbye.

"Okay, I gotta ask," Nancy said. "What's up with Iris repeating everything everyone says?"

Shane gathered his thoughts, about to give a detailed psychological explanation, when Becky blurted out, "Echolalia."

Caught off guard, Shane smiled at Becky.

"Echo what?" Nancy and Tommy asked at the same time.

Becky replied, "Echolalia. It's when someone repeats what others say. It's part of how they communicate. A kid in my grade has it, and everyone in our class is just used to it. He can't help it. It's kind of like when you see someone yawn, and then you have to yawn too? That's how our teachers explained it to us. It's not a big deal."

Shane nodded, impressed with Becky's simple, matter-of-fact explanation, "Sometimes people on the autism spectrum have it. I'm not saying she has autism—I'm not *diagnosing*," he added, to be clear.

Nancy said, "Sometimes it feels like she might be mocking us when she does it, but then you look at her, and it's clear she isn't. She's the sweetest thing."

Becky said, "No, she isn't doing it on purpose."

Trish said, "I think Iris is cool. I love her unique sense of style, but I want to teach her to do makeup. She has gorgeous eyes. We could really make them pop with the right products."

"I like her too," Becky said. "She's very artsy."

"Echolalia," Nancy said, adding, "you learn something new every day."

CHAPTER 16

Team Buster

Nancy, Iris, and Trish sat in the gazebo, brainstorming. What could they do to help Buster stop barking up at the trees?

Gretchen, walking back from chastising a young couple for not picking up their dog's poop, said, "For one, he needs more exercise, and maybe some stimulation for his brain."

"But he has no interest in running around the park like other dogs," Iris said. "He just stands there, barking."

"Well, then *you* take him for a run."

Iris had never run in her life. She'd always been profoundly unathletic.

"I'm afraid I'm not much of a runner," she said, doubtfully.

Gretchen handed Iris her business card. "Call me, if you want any help with him."

Just then, Tommy came around the corner entering the gazebo, glistening in sweat. He'd heard the end of their conversation and said, "He can do the loop around the park with me and Rocky if he wants."

"You would do that? Take him with you?" Iris asked.

"Why not?" Tommy shrugged. "The more the merrier! Let's try it and see how it goes!"

"Let's try it and see how it goes!" Iris repeated.

Gretchen nodded, impressed.

Trish smiled at Tommy, nearly swooning.

Two days later, Iris watched nervously as Tommy ran off with Buster and Rocky for a five-mile run. She walked laps with Trish and Gigi to pass the time. Trish confided in Iris that she had a wicked crush on Tommy. Iris beamed, shoving her glasses back up the bridge of her nose as she kept pace with Trish. She was honored to be in on Trish's secret. This was so romantic! And Iris was *thrilled* to be taking part in girl talk.

Buster was so out of shape he could barely keep up with Tommy and Rocky. They wound up cutting the run short and walking the last two miles back to the dog enclosures.

When they arrived, hot and panting, Trish pressed the button on the doggie water fountain with her foot, glancing at Tommy's taut abs as she did so. Rocky and Buster each took a long drink. Rocky ran off to greet his pal, Henry. And then, for the first time ever, Buster came into the gazebo and lay down at Iris's feet. She raised her eyebrows and looked at Nancy who was smiling back at her.

"You're a good kid, Tommy," Nancy said, nodding approvingly at him.

Tommy grinned, and shrugged his shoulders dramatically, tipping his head to the side and clasping his hands under his chin like a schoolboy.

"Aw, shucks, y'all." He batted his eyelashes at Nancy.

She laughed and said, "Don't push it, Tommy."

Trish looked at Iris conspiratorially. Iris grinned back, Trish's secret safe with her.

That weekend, Iris got together with Gretchen to discuss Buster's bad habit. They wound up grabbing dinner together. The next night, Trish invited her to see a movie. When she got home that night, Iris happily paced around her apartment, listening to music, her arm joyfully conducting a private orchestra. She was filled to the brim from recent happenings with new friends.

CHAPTER 17

Choco's Florida Adventure

Tommy and Rocky took Buster with them three times a week for the next couple of months, but this day, he'd texted her to say he wasn't up for their usual run. When he and Rocky came in through the gate, Tommy's eyes were red. His hair clung to his head, greasy. He wore a stained T-shirt.

Nancy asked, "What's going on, Tommy? You look like you've been hit by a bus!"

"Worse," Tommy said. "Gina broke up with me."

Choco had been sitting on Iris's lap enjoying a full-body massage. Iris paused, glancing at Trish, who looked anything but sad to hear the news.

"Aw, Tommy," Nancy said. "Having your heart broken really stinks. I'm sorry, buddy. I have certainly been there. Did she sleep with your best friend like my piece of shit Anthony did?"

Everyone turned to look at Nancy.

"Don't feel sorry for me." She waved them off. "I'm better off with Teddy. Sure, like Anthony, he's lazy, and he snores, and he passes copious amounts of gas, but at least he's loyal. As long as I have my rotisserie chicken from Publix, my Salem Lights, the Yankees on TV, and old Ted here, I'm doing just fine."

Nancy continued, "Do you want to talk about it, Tommy?"

Tommy said, "Not really."

Trish tilted her head and gave him what she hoped looked like a sympathetic smile. Choco hopped down from Iris's lap and up onto Tommy's.

Nancy said, "Choco always knows who needs cheering up. Are you a little therapy dog? You little hot dog? Are you a love bug? Are you so friendly?"

"Mayor of Lake Woof," Tommy said, letting out a sad sigh. "Friendliest dog you'll ever meet."

He closed his eyes and slumped on the bench, stroking Choco's ears.

Sitting in the gazebo, Ann chimed in. She was freshly showered and recently had her roots done. She was looking a bit more like herself.

"Sometimes he's *too* friendly," Ann said.

"How can a dog be too friendly?" Becky asked. She and her dogs had been at Lake Woof for two hours already, and she was waiting for Bruce to pick them up.

Hoping to take Tommy's mind off his troubles, Ann began telling the story of Choco's Florida adventure.

When Liam was 10 years old and Choco was two, she decided to take them camping at a local state park. She'd been intimidated by the idea of setting up a tent on her own, so had rented a small camper van. There were plenty of kids Liam's age at the campsite, most of them boys. Ann got to lie in a hammock and read books while Liam and Choco ran wild. Choco had rarely been off leash in the city and was ecstatic running from campsite to campsite, making friends, darting into the woods after chipmunks and squirrels and running back out to find Liam when he failed to catch them. They stayed four nights, swimming and hiking and making obligatory s'mores around the campfire with the other families. Ann had visions of possibly returning every year, but when it was time to go, they couldn't find Choco.

All the adults and children searched for the missing Dachshund, walking every trail, calling his name. Liam did not hide his tears in front of the other boys and became more frantic by the hour. Where could he be? Was he hurt somewhere? Had he been attacked by another animal? Bitten by a snake somewhere in the woods? Was he scared?

At 10 p.m., a park ranger came to talk to them. They'd searched everywhere. Addressing Ann, he said, "Ma'am, this is why there are leash laws in the state parks." He said they would keep a lookout and let them know if anyone saw him. Ann and Liam, horrified by the thought of leaving without Choco, decided to stay. The next day the children put up fliers all over the park. Two mothers plastered local social media with Choco's photo, and they called all the animal shelters. Finally, Ann had to admit defeat. They left the park two days later, dejected.

Back home, Liam couldn't sleep without Choco. He was so heartsick he missed a week of school. Ann cuddled him at night, holding him and wiping his tears.

And then Ann got a phone call from an area code she didn't recognize.

A woman on the line said, "We saw a post on Facebook. I think we might have your dog. Can we text you a photo to confirm?"

Seeing the photo, Ann shrieked, "Oh my God! Oh my God! You found him! Thank you! Thank you! You have no idea how much my son has been suffering!" She looked at Liam who had tears streaming down his face. "Please give me your address, and we will come over right away to get him!"

"He's okay. He's okay. He's okay," Liam repeated softly, rocking forward and back, prayer hands at his chest, thanking God.

The woman on the line said, "We'd been hiking and found him all alone at Davis Mountain State Park. He followed us to the parking lot and jumped right into the car and up onto my partner's lap as we were heading out."

Ann said, "Yes, he's always been very friendly."

"We waited around for a while and asked a few people if he was their dog, and no one claimed him. We thought he'd been abandoned."

"Well, thank you for picking him up. He certainly wasn't abandoned. Can we come get him please?" Ann asked.

"You know, you really shouldn't let dogs off leash in state parks. He didn't even have a collar on. It's very irresponsible. You never know what could have happened to him. We've become very fond of him, and my spouse isn't sure we should give him back.

She's very concerned that he, you know, was running around on his own."

Ann felt anger rising in her belly but kept levelheaded, her Building Bridges training serving her now.

"Can you please give me your name and address so we can pick him up?" Ann asked.

"Sure, but we're in Central Florida, about nine hours away from Haberland City."

"You took my son's dog *nine hours away?*" Ann said, seething through clenched teeth.

"Hey, lady, you're lucky your dog isn't dead. We could have taken him to a shelter or something. Or he could have been lost in the woods. We've been taking *very* good care of him."

Ann realized this woman could hang up and block her, and they'd never see Choco again.

She thought quickly and appealed to the woman, telling her the story of Choco, and how Liam had dreamed of him for years. How her sweet fatherless little boy hadn't been able to sleep without his dog. She told her how much Liam's heart was breaking without Choco.

"I see," the woman said, her tone softening. "So, his name is Choco? We've been calling him Davis, after the park. *Davis,* get it?"

Ann had already taken time off for the camping trip and an extra week to support Liam. She couldn't drive nine hours to get Choco this week.

Ann played the women like a hostage negotiator, buying time until she could get there the following weekend, willing them to stop falling more in love with Liam's dog. She managed to get their names and gain their friendship on Facebook.

For a week, Ann trod lightly, watching anxiously as they posted pictures of "Davis" at the beach. Davis at Starbucks. Davis snuggled up in their bed. She held her breath. She countered with photos on her own wall, posting the story of Choco and Liam, and tagging the women who had found Choco in the park. She knew they (and all their friends) would see her posts, and she gushed about what good Samaritans they were for taking such good care of *Liam's* dog.

When Ann and Liam finally arrived to pick him up, Choco, wearing a new collar, tackled Liam the moment they opened the door. Boy and dog wept with joy, rolling around on the ground. Two women stood in the doorway, crying.

They had a bag of toys and treats for Choco to take with him. They included a small photo album of all the places they'd been in the two weeks since they'd kidnapped him. A dog park, a parade, a beach party where Choco wore a Hawaiian shirt and a fedora. His nails had been trimmed, and he'd been freshly bathed. He'd been to a child's birthday party and a doggie event at a local library.

In each photo, Choco looked relaxed and happy. He'd been living it up while Liam suffered. Ann hated these women.

She thanked them again, and as they were leaving, one of them said, in a scolding tone, "Next time, be more careful."

Ann offered a tight smile and hurried Liam and Choco to the Volvo, as the women cried, "Bye, Davis! We love you, Davis!"

In the car, Liam held onto Choco tightly. Ann patted his leg as she steered onto the highway for the long drive home. Tears of relief dripped down Liam's face, and Choco licked them off.

As soon as they got home, Ann blocked the women on Facebook.

In the gazebo, Nancy, Tommy, Trish and Iris let out a collective exhale.

Becky said, "Oh my God, Ann!"

All eyes turned from Ann to Choco, who had moved to Trish's lap during the telling of the story. He was blissed out, getting a full-body scratch from her long fingernails.

Tommy looked from Choco, to Trish, as if seeing her for the first time. She was so pretty. She smiled softly at him, and he smiled back. Across the park, Rocky and Gigi happily rolled on their backs in the mud at the bottom of the dirt mountain.

Just then, Bruce pulled up. Becky called her dogs and loaded them into the truck before finally heading home.

CHAPTER 18

Always the Bad Guy

Mr. Damon had curated an art show, and Becky wanted to go, but Bruce said no. She was so sick of her father.

"Fine, *Bruce*. I guess it's okay with you if I never go anywhere besides the dog park, and never have any friends," Becky said, stomping off toward her bedroom.

Bruce flew across the living room and pinned her to the wall by her neck with one hand, his other raised to strike. His face inches from hers, he seethed, "You call me *Dad*, or you call me *Sir*. You do not call me by my name. I will not have you turn into a mouthy little bitch like your mother. You hear?"

Becky felt her father's hot breath as his hand hovered above her head.

She held his eye. She did not answer with, "Yes, sir," or even a nod. She glared, as if willing him to hit her. Becky often thought being hit might be easier than his emotional abuse. A hit you could quantify. It might leave a physical mark. Maybe she could even report it to someone, a teacher? The cops?

Later, when they pulled into the dog park, Shane was in the parking lot with Blue.

He heard Bruce say, "I mean it, Becky. Every day, you're more like your mother, and that is no compliment."

"Can you just leave my mother alone?" Becky snapped back at him.

Shane stepped in and said, "Hey, can I help with anything here? You okay, Becky?"

"I would advise you to mind your own fucking business," Bruce snapped at Shane.

"Dad! He's trying to help. Stop it."

Bruce bellowed, "Oh, sure, Becky, I'm always the bad guy. Don't you ever fucking forget I'm the one who stayed. It was your *mother* who ran off on us, who started a new family with some other guy. I devoted my whole life to you. A little fucking gratitude would be nice once in a while."

Wayne had just finished putting his dogs in the back of the van when he came around to the driver's side, noting the commotion.

Bruce glared at him. "What the fuck are *you* looking at?"

Wayne's fists clenched, and he set his jaw. He stared long and hard at Bruce. Finally, Bruce turned away from him. Wayne took a breath and silently reminded himself, "*Mind your own goddamn business. It ain't worth it.*"

Bruce got into his truck and on the way out rolled down his window and yelled to Becky, "I'll pick you up when I damn well feel like it," then sped away.

Wayne shook his head and got in his van. *Real tough guy*, he thought. *Damn shame that little girl has to put up with him.*

Shane and Blue walked with Becky and the huskies toward the fenced enclosure.

Becky knew Bruce was heading to Malone's Tavern. It had become his home away from home in the last year since Katie died. Becky glanced over her shoulder, watching her father's truck get smaller and smaller as he headed out of the park.

"I fucking hate you," she said through clenched teeth.

Shane asked Becky if she wanted to walk some laps with him and Blue.

"Okay, but I don't feel like talking," she said.

"You don't have to," he said.

Nancy, Ed, and Tommy had been sitting in the gazebo and couldn't help but hear Bruce's chaos.

"Imagine, *he's* the good parent?" Nancy said.

"Poor kid," Tommy said.

Nancy added, "Now, I don't have kids, but I wonder what was up with her mother? How can a parent just abandon their own child?"

It was a question Becky asked herself constantly since her mother gave Bruce custody years ago. When Katie moved away with her new husband and Becky's little brothers, Becky concluded it was somehow her fault, and that she was terribly unlovable. Though her mom had come to visit her every other weekend without fail, Becky never shook the feeling that Katie took the kids she loved the most and left her behind with Bruce.

Tommy shook his head, joining Nancy in her judgment of Becky's mom.

"I don't know, Nance, but they do it. My old man left me and my mom when I was three years old. I don't remember him at all, and she won't even talk about him. Last year I put my spit on 23 and Me, and a distant cousin reached out to me a couple weeks ago. I'm thinking about meeting her. Maybe she can tell me about my bio dad, or knows where he is?"

Ed said, "Bio dad?"

Tommy said, "Yeah, the guy who knocked up my ma."

Ed cleared his throat. "Tommy, do you think that's a good idea? I mean, you could be opening a can of worms."

"I don't know," Tommy said. "I'm curious."

Nancy said, "He might not be worth meeting."

Ed cleared his throat, got up off the bench, and said, "I feel like walking."

Ed wished he could walk by himself. He needed to clear his head, but Tommy joined him, followed by Henry and Rocky.

Ed was silent for a couple of laps, Nancy's question repeating in his head. "How could anyone abandon their child?" How had *he* done it? The son he left behind would be in his forties now. Ed hadn't seen the boy since he was a toddler.

CHAPTER 19

Ed

Ed was 19 when his new girlfriend became pregnant. Sabrina had been just 17. He'd already been living on his own for four years. After his parents split, he'd chosen to live with his dad. Ed felt sorry for him after his mother had kicked him out, but soon he was taking the full brunt of his father's alcoholic tirades.

After Ed moved in with his father, his mother moved his grandmother in to help with the younger kids, and there was no longer any room for Ed in his childhood home. Not that his pride would have allowed him to come back or ask his mother for help.

Ed was physically strong and a hard worker. He dropped out of high school and took hard labor jobs for local contractors who paid him under the table. He helped build houses, and he was smart, picking up skills quickly. There was never a lack of work. One day he would take all he learned and build his own home with his own two hands. It would have gleaming copper plumbing and radiant heat in the floors. But at 15, he rented a little studio tucked into a row of garages people rented to store cars in the winter. He had a stove, a bed, a small shower, and a guitar he'd picked up at a garage sale for five bucks. Not much else.

Ed taught himself to play a bit in the lonely hours he was not at work. He found a flier for a jam session at a local coffee shop and decided to check it out one evening. This was where he met his child's mother. Her brothers were guitar players a few years older than Ed. They took him under their wing. They taught him how to really play, not just pick out chords here or there. He was a quick learner, and he was quiet and polite. They liked Ed. The three played acoustically together, and he found he could sing harmonies blending seamlessly with the two of them. Making music with them required very little effort; it was pure joy. They mostly did covers of other musicians, The Beatles, Simon and Garfunkel, etc. Ed had written some of his own stuff but was too shy to ever share it.

He'd already been on his own for almost four years when they stopped playing open mics at the coffee shop and began doing gigs at a local bar, getting paid.

Sabrina was pretty with bright blue eyes, and long, strawberry-blonde hair. She had a slim figure and wore halter tops that showed her bare freckled arms. When she was 17, she finally convinced her parents to let her go to the bar to see her brothers perform. Ed knew his bandmates had a sister, but in his mind, she was a little kid. When he met her, he was surprised at how pretty she was, and how grown up she was, but barely gave her a second thought.

Sabrina could not take her eyes off Ed. She focused on his forearms, so strong from all the physical labor he did, his shoulders, broad from lifting concrete. She liked his bright blue eyes and noticed his square jawline. Something about the way he concentrated on his guitar was so vulnerable and sexy, unlike her own brothers who just seemed ridiculously goofy to her. She started showing up more often, and her brothers would give her rides home. She even convinced them to pay her a little cash for helping set up and break down their sets.

One Friday after a gig, they all went out to Denny's for late-night food. Sabrina made sure to sit next to Ed. They both ordered the Grand Slam breakfast.

The young men talked about the gig they just did, and Sabrina interjected as much as she could. She was cute, Ed thought. A bit sassy and sarcastic. She mentioned she worked at the donut shop near his apartment.

Ed had just scooped a forkful of eggs into his mouth when Sabrina leaned her knee into his, forcefully enough for him to know it wasn't an accident. If it were, she would have pulled away quickly, and probably been embarrassed. But she left it there, pressing. He looked up at her brothers across the table. They were oblivious to the knee situation going on underneath. Ed swallowed his eggs without pulling his own knee away and felt his heart begin to beat faster.

She showed up at his door that Sunday morning with donuts and coffee. She had done some digging and found out where he lived. He opened the door in boxer shorts. He was groggy, this, his one day of the week to sleep in. The bright sun almost blinded him, as he rubbed his eyes, and ran a hand through his hair. She stood in the doorway looking at his smooth chest, his shoulders.

"I brought you some breakfast," she said. "Can I come in?"

"Yeah," he said. "Sure."

He shut the door behind them.

Ed excused himself to use the bathroom where he looked himself over in the mirror. He brushed his teeth and splashed water on his face.

Sabrina set the donuts and coffee down on the small kitchen counter. She looked around his studio apartment. It was tidy, but the decades-old indoor/outdoor carpet was musty, and the grime on the only window muted the bright morning sun attempting to shine through it.

She opened the box and took out a glazed donut. When he came out, she handed it to him, then looked him straight in the eye as she licked the glaze off her fingertips. He took a bite, staring at her, wondering if he was dreaming. He swallowed the bite, took a gulp of coffee, and set the cup back down on the table.

Sabrina had only had sex with one boy before, but she came at him fast and with confidence. Throwing her arms around him, she began to kiss his mouth, his shoulders. She breathed in the smell of his chest and slid her hand down below his waist.

Ed felt dizzy. He still wasn't sure he wasn't dreaming.

He picked her up, and she straddled him with her legs, kissing his neck. He set her onto his bed. His breathing was heavy. As he stood over her, her brothers' faces flashed through his mind.

"Sabrina, are you sure about this?" Ed asked.

She reached into her back jeans pocket and pulled out a string of condoms she'd stolen from one of their dresser drawers. She smiled at him, and said, "Totally sure."

For Ed, these moments with Sabrina were sublime. He'd been so lonely since being out on his own. He had no friends to hang out with. Everyone his age was still in school. And he was too young to go out to bars with his coworkers. He'd quietly gotten his GED when he turned 18 and had just kept his head down and his nose clean. But he ached for friendship and for physical affection. He'd had a couple of one-night stands in the past couple of years, but nothing he felt proud of, and with no one he'd ever want to see again.

Sometimes he had to stop himself from crying when they were intimate, the physical touch threatening to knock down the walls he'd built up around himself for protection. He'd had to be so tough for so long.

Ed and Sabrina explored every inch of each other's bodies. Their time together felt like a wild beautiful storm. And then, just two months in, lightning struck them hard.

Sabrina showed up one day, pounding on his door; when he opened it, she thrust the stick into his face.

"What's this?" he said, his heart sinking. He was pretty sure he knew what it was.

"I'm pregnant, you idiot," she said, looking at him like it was his fault, like he'd done this to her on purpose.

She paced the floor, eyebrows knitted together, biting at the cuticle of her thumb. "My parents are going to kill me," she said. Then, looking sharply at him, she added, "My brothers are going to kill *you*."

He winced at the thought of her brothers knowing and studied her face looking for a hint of what she planned to do. But it seemed she didn't have a plan, and everything he suggested was shot down.

He asked if she were considering an abortion, and she drew back, offended.

"I'm not going to *kill* it."

"Okay." He nodded, knowing it was her choice.

"What about adoption?"

"How do you know it isn't going to end up with some psycho who will abuse it?"

He nodded, again, hearing her out, the guilty knots in his stomach tightening.

A month went by, and still, nothing was decided. He offered to marry her, and she said, "I'm fucking 17! I don't want to be married! And besides, it's not like you even really want to."

"Okay, okay," he said, backing off, feeling helpless to resolve the situation.

Finally, she told him she was going to keep the baby. Since she was only 17 and wanted freedom to still be a kid, he would have the baby half the week; they would split custody 50-50. That was her plan. Sabrina had decided his life for him.

Her parents were mortified but agreed to support her. Her brothers told him not to come around anymore. They kicked him out of the group. They'd been his only friends.

Sabrina stopped coming to his apartment. She only called to tell him what was what. Ed had never been lonelier than those last months waiting for the baby to arrive. Finally, their child was born, a healthy boy. Her brothers convinced Sabrina to name him Eric, after Eric Clapton.

Ed found himself at 20, with 50-50 custody of Eric. He got a secondhand highchair and a playpen he used as a crib. He learned how to change diapers and make bottles. He worked double time his days on, so he could work just four days, and have the days he was responsible for Eric off. He had no idea what he was doing and no support. His mother was already working nights and raising his younger siblings. He was too proud to ask her for help, and he didn't want to be a burden.

Ed went on like this for almost two years, trying to be a good dad for Eric. He had no social life. He let on to no one how stressed he was. There were no support groups for single young fathers. There was no one in the world Ed felt he could talk to.

Every time he picked Eric up from Sabrina's, she was hostile. She resented being a teen mom and blamed him for it, having forgotten it was she who had come on to him. Her parents were cold to him as well. And her brothers didn't speak to him at all. Sabrina's older sister was the only one who seemed to have any compassion for him. She would sometimes be the one to bring baby Eric to the car for hand-offs, and more than once, she apologized for how poorly Sabrina and the rest of her family were treating him.

Snapping the baby into the car seat one afternoon, she said, "You're doing a good job, Ed."

Her kindness sustained him more than she would ever know.

Ed held baby Eric, fed him, comforted him, took care of his physical needs. There were moments of true bonding when Eric fell asleep on his chest, but Ed was always so anxious, afraid he was screwing things up. There was no one to offer encouragement, no one to hand the baby off to when he was frustrated or when his feelings of overwhelm and exhaustion became too much. He felt trapped. Still, he kept trying.

He'd dress Eric in a cute outfit and bring him to his mom's house for Thanksgiving, or Easter. Sabrina would show up in the middle of dinner making a scene, yanking the baby out, saying she needed him to come home with her, now. Something about the baby being away from her on holidays bothered her. Sabrina had always gotten her way and felt entitled to take him whenever she wanted.

Sabrina would announce at the drop of a hat that she was switching days if something came up she wanted to do, forcing Ed to scramble to rearrange his work schedule, angering his foreman.

Sabrina talked disparagingly about Ed all over town, so anywhere he went, people treated him as if he were a jerk. It was as if people thought he got her pregnant on purpose, or that he somehow wasn't supporting her or the baby.

Eric had his second birthday. Ed was not invited to the party at Sabrina's parents' house.

Then one day, Sabrina showed up at Ed's apartment with Eric. She announced they were getting back together. She'd brought an overnight bag. She'd been in a fight with her parents and told them on her way out, "I'm taking the baby, and you'll never see him again."

They'd hardly been "together" as a couple even before Eric was born two years ago. It had been sex, not a relationship. Now she wanted to play house.

At Ed's, she criticized how he did everything. How he changed a diaper. How he made and washed the bottles. Everything he did was stupid and wrong in her eyes, and she could do it better. Two months went by. He took care of Eric when she went out with friends after work. She'd come in late, and clunk around, waking them both up, not considering Ed needed to be up early for work, or that the baby needed his sleep.

To this day, Ed didn't know how long he would have lasted, if he hadn't woken up one morning frantically scratching his pubic hair. Sabrina had given him crabs.

She had the nerve to deny it at first, but he wasn't having it. He hadn't slept with anyone else, and he raised his voice, calling her out on it. It was the first time he'd ever yelled at her, and she began to cry, admitting she'd been sleeping with another guy in the two months since they'd been living together. She'd done it while he was home with the baby.

He couldn't take it anymore.

"GET OUT!" he bellowed. "GET THE FUCK OUT OF HERE, SABRINA!"

She gathered up her purse, and Eric, and repeated the threat she'd given her parents.

"You know, Ed, I can take this baby, and you'll never see him again. You think you are so great? You're Mr. Perfect? Fuck you."

She slammed the door on the way out. He could hear Eric crying as Sabrina put him in the car.

Ed paced around, his emotions so roiled up he started to cry. Could he really deal with Sabrina for the rest of his life? He scratched his crotch, then picked up a plate off his little kitchen table and threw it against the wall, where it shattered into pieces. He'd have to find a doctor to get help for the crabs. It was all so embarrassing. It was all so impossible.

At just 22 years old, he hadn't time to process his own childhood traumas. He knew he loved Eric, but he could hardly feel it because he was always exhausted and overwhelmed. He knew he had to do something drastic, or he would be tied to this selfish girl forever. He knew Sabrina's family would take care of Eric. He knew she had support.

The next day, after seeing a doctor at a walk-in clinic who prescribed a special shampoo, he enlisted in the military. He made the decision in a panic, and while he was panicking, he also went to the courthouse and numbly signed his parental rights away, to Sabrina. He would regret it later, but in that moment, he needed to get away from this town, and away from everything that hurt him. It felt like life or death, and Ed chose his own life.

Sabrina couldn't believe it when he told her. "Don't you care about Eric at all? How could you give up your right to be his father?" she shrieked and began sobbing.

Ed sat stone-faced, numb. The decision had been made.

She turned and stomped out of his apartment. He didn't get to say goodbye to his son.

Military life was a great relief to Ed. He knew what to expect. There was order and predictability. He followed the rules and did a good job. Hard workers like him were noticed and rewarded. He moved quickly up the ranks. While in the military, Ed went on four deployments, loving each one of them. They were the adventures of his lifetime. Because of his skills in building structures, he was in charge of setting up temporary barracks. He was never put at the front line. Ed found other musicians to jam with in the long boring hours of downtime.

Low-grade guilt hung around him like a dormant virus, but he kept it at bay by keeping busy. At night in the barracks, the love for his child, a longing for Eric, would sneak up on him as he tried to go to sleep. His throat would tighten when he imagined his son. How big was he now? What was he doing? His body ached to hold him. Ed would swallow the lump in his throat and push his feelings down deep. This was not the place to cry.

Meanwhile, Sabrina milked the situation for sympathy. She told their whole town how Ed abandoned her and the baby. How he got her pregnant and never even cared. She never mentioned the two years Ed had put in trying. She didn't tell people about the support checks she received every month of his life until Eric turned 21. Ed had never missed one of them.

When Eric was four, Sabrina's sister sent him a letter. It said Sabrina had married "in ceremony" (not legally so as not to forfeit Ed's financial support) a guy she knew from high school. They were raising the child to believe this guy was Eric's father.

Up until then, Ed thought one day he might be able to explain everything to Eric. Now, that plan was moot. He didn't feel he had the right to disrupt the child's life after what he'd done. For the rest of his son's childhood, he had no further contact with Sabrina. He feared if Eric ever found out the truth, he would hate him.

Ed had a couple of long-term relationships, but never married and had no other children. Deep down, a part of him thought he didn't deserve it.

Tommy snapped his fingers in front of Ed's face.

"Hey, Ed, where'd ya go?" he laughed.

Ed startled, shaking off the memories. He looked at Rocky and Henry frolicking out in front of them.

Tommy said, "So why do you think it might stir up a can of worms? What if it worked out great? What if my bio-dad is a good guy?"

Ed said, "Do you really think someone who abandons his son could be a good guy?"

Tommy replied, "Truthfully, I don't know. Maybe he was a good guy who was going through a hard time? Or maybe he's an asshole. Or maybe—" Tommy stopped walking and turned toward Ed. "Maybe—" Tommy dropped his head and looked at his shoes. He took a second to compose himself. "I mean, I've always been *a lot.* I was already three years old when he left. Like, he knew me a little already, ya know?" He looked up at Ed, bit his lip.

"Maybe he just didn't like me?"

Ed winced. He let out a long exhale.

"Some things are just not easily explained, Tommy! Some things don't make sense as they are happening and never make sense again." Ed's voice got louder and more intense. He took Tommy by the shoulders and almost pleaded, "Don't assume your bio dad didn't love you. It might have been an impossible situation!" And then, in a gesture so uncharacteristic of Ed it surprised them both, he pulled Tommy into a strong hug,

"It wasn't your fault. You are a *very lovable* kid," he said into Tommy's ear.

To Tommy it was like hearing the voice of God.

He slumped onto Ed's shoulder and began to sob.

Nancy sat in the gazebo taking note. "I wonder what's going on over there?" she said, pointing to Ed and Tommy across the green space. Ann and Iris turned to look in their direction.

They watched the men release from a long embrace. Ed took a handkerchief from his jacket pocket, carefully unfolded it, and offered it to Tommy who shook his head, refusing it. Ed then used it to blow his own nose. The two resumed walking, and Tommy wiped his nose on the sleeve of his hoodie.

After a while, Ed said, "Did I ever tell you I used to play guitar?"

Tommy said, "No way?"

Ed replied, "Way."

Rocky and Henry walked 20 paces ahead, tails wagging.

Nancy said, "Looks like they worked it out, whatever it was."

Ann focused on Tommy. He was 25, not so much older than Liam. She wondered what her son would have looked like, would have been doing at 25 years old? He'd have been done with college, probably enjoying his first "real" job.

Thinking of Liam, tears began to form in Ann's eyes. Her ache, an endless abyss. She gathered up Choco abruptly, said goodbye, and made her way out of the park.

CHAPTER 20

The Glasses

When Ann informed the college she was taking the summer semester off, she didn't really care if they let her go. It had been over six months, and she could still barely get herself together to take Choco to Lake Woof. She felt no motivation to teach. She'd have a few good days, then get blindsided with grief. Suicide fantasies began creeping in again.

She stood on her tiptoes in the hall entryway, reaching up, and felt around on the top of the coat rack/shoe/bench unit for a plastic dog poop bag to take with her. Her hand brushed against something hard, and she pulled down a dark glasses case. Liam's sunglasses. He'd taken to wearing aviators with blue lenses last year. She dropped the case onto the bench as a fresh wave of grief washed over her.

Dropping the leash, she slid to the floor. Tears came, as she sat in a heap, slumped against the wall. Choco climbed onto her lap.

Clutching the glasses case in one hand, she rested her other hand on Choco's back. Her eyes were always so puffy and swollen she wondered if maybe she'd damaged them for good. There were new lines on her face that didn't seem to be going away. Every time she thought she was through the worst of the grief, it showed itself again. There would always be something. Every new scab barely formed, constantly ripped off by memory. Her longing for Liam would never end. Ann began to sob. Chest heaving, she couldn't catch her breath.

Choco hopped off her lap and made skittling noises against the tile floor with his toenails as he danced around her. After the tears began to subside, he sniffed her face and licked her cheeks. He stared up at her with his big dark soulful eyes. He tilted his head as if he had a question.

"Oh, Choco," she said, "how are we going to do this?" His toenails click-click-clicked into the living room, and he came back with his green ball, dropping it beside her. He play-bowed and looked up expectantly.

Ann said, "I don't feel like playing, Choco, but you're such a good boy."

She pulled him in close, kissed the top of his head, and stared off into the distance, absentmindedly stroking his ears. He settled onto her lap, and her nerves began to calm. She recalled how Liam used to rub Choco's velvety ears across his lips to fall asleep at night, his baby blanket only truly given up once Choco arrived.

Ann got up and walked into the bathroom. She held onto the sink and took some deep breaths. She washed her face and held a cold cloth to her eyes. Every so often, her lungs heaved a shuddering sigh.

Ann decided to skip the dog park. It was all too much.

Walking toward the living room, she noticed her purse lying on the floor where she had fallen apart. She went to hang it up and again saw the glasses case. It was then Ann noticed the designer label on the side and remembered them. These were *women's* glasses. Readers. She'd splurged on them last year. She'd been feeling frumpy and went a little edgy. She chose bold red horn-rimmed glasses, much bigger than she'd normally pick, much different from her regular, more subdued frames.

Liam had been with her. "Go for it, Mom," he said, encouraging her to buy them.

Liam must have carried them in from the car and set them on the high shelf in the hall. She would never have put them way up there. Ann had forgotten she ever bought them.

For a moment, Ann stood stunned, glasses case in one hand, dog leash in the other, poor Choco wondering if they'd ever get out the door. How on earth had she cried so hard over a pair of her *own* glasses? Ann felt ridiculous and started to laugh.

A rush flowed through her entire body. It was as if Liam were right there laughing with her. As if he'd put the glasses up where she couldn't reach them to play a joke on her.

You finally found them, Mom.

It felt like millions of carbonated bubbles flowing through her. The sun poured in through the side window of the foyer, and she imagined Liam's voice:

"You look for me everywhere, but I am right here, Mom. The only thing different is my form. You make your own meaning out of everything. The glasses—you made them mean loss, you made them mean I was gone from you, but I'm not. Cry every tear you need to, but know I am here, waiting for you to join me when you feel joy. You'll find me in your laughter. Crying over your own glasses is freakin' hilarious, Mom. Admit it."

Ann looked again at the designer glasses case in her hand. She threw back her head and cackled almost maniacally. She thought she might be going insane, and then laughed about that too.

Liam continued in her mind. *"You'll never find me in sadness because I am pure positive energy now. I can't even access sorrow from where I am. Find me, feel me, in joy. That's where we'll connect."*

"Oh, Liam," she said. "Why did you have to leave me? I want you here with me. I miss you so much."

"Our souls agreed—this or something like this is how it would unfold. If not a car accident, it would have been something else. So, stop blaming yourself for making me come home for Thanksgiving break."

Ann sucked in her breath.

"And stop dreaming of ending your life sooner. There is nowhere to escape to. All that would be avoided would be right there for you to pick up next time around. There are those who still need you and many lives you will touch. You're not done, and you've not even met all the people who will love you, Mom. You can do this. I'm right here with you, closer than you've been imagining. I love you. Now please get Choco outside. Little bruh is so confused."

Choco stood looking at Ann holding the leash, waiting. His tail, thumping against the floor.

Ann took the readers out of the case. She walked to the hall mirror and put them on, looking at herself. They *did* look edgy. She took them off and tucked them back into the case, dropping them into her purse.

Ann blew her nose, then clicked Choco's leash onto his collar. She took in a deep breath, exhaled, and headed out to the dog park.

CHAPTER 21

Ann and Becky

Bruce pulled up to Lake Woof, dropped Becky off with the dogs, and peeled out of the parking lot. The dog park was mostly empty, just Nancy and Ann this late afternoon. Teddy lay in the gazebo snoozing, and Choco was out at the far end of the green space sniffing.

The huskies ran across the field to greet Choco. They sniffed his butt, and Choco went onto his back, submissively. They tired of him quickly and ran off on their own. After a while, Choco came back to the gazebo and put his paws up on Becky's lap. She lifted him up and began petting him.

Nancy said, "That little sausage sure is a love bug."

Becky sighed.

"How you doin', kiddo?" Nancy asked. "Why so glum?"

"Oh, nothing. Just my dad is a jerk," Becky said. "The usual."

Well, yeah, there's that, Nancy thought. But what she said was, "I'm sorry you're having a bad day. Did you get in a fight?"

"I was supposed to go to the mall to meet some kids from school, but instead he dropped me off here for God knows how long, to punish me."

"Ah," Nancy said. "You mean you'd rather go to the mall with a bunch of good-looking teenagers than sit here and talk to a couple of old ladies all afternoon?" she added.

Nancy laughed at her own joke, which got her coughing.

Becky smiled.

A new dog entered the park, and Ruger charged toward it, baring his teeth.

Becky yelled, "Ruger! Knock it off!" He didn't listen, so she walked over and grabbed him by the collar and gave him a swat on the butt before letting him go again and heading back into the gazebo.

The dog's owners quickly called their dog. They exited and went to the small dog section instead.

Nancy thought to herself, *The two older huskies never have a problem, but the young one is trouble. He's so easily agitated.*

"Before you got here, Becky, Ann was telling me more about Choco. Her son Liam dreamed of him when he was a little boy. He drew pictures of him, already had a name for him, talked about him all the time before she finally surprised him on his eighth birthday."

Ann nodded, smiling at Becky. "It was the best day of my life, aside from the day Liam was born," she sighed.

"Cool," Becky said, a bit disinterested.

Wayne showed up, and Choco ran the fence with Thor and Roach. When he was leaving, Becky walked into the parking lot with her backpack on. As she approached him, he looked at her cautiously.

"I have something for you," Becky said, unzipping her bag and fishing her sketchpad out. She opened it, flipped through, and ripped out a page, handing it to him.

Wayne took the paper and studied it. Becky had sketched a portrait of Wayne and his dogs. He looked up at Becky.

"You drew this?" he asked.

She nodded, biting her lip.

"You and your dogs are some of the most interesting ones at Lake Woof," she said.

Wayne looked at the drawing again. He carried no cell phone or camera and had no recent photos of himself.

"That was real nice of you, kid," he said. "I appreciate you giving me this."

Becky shrugged and said, "It's no big deal."

As she walked back to the enclosure, she looked over her shoulder and saw Wayne smiling down at the drawing in his hands. She beamed, feeling proud.

Two hours went by, and Bruce did not show up. Nancy had to take Teddy home for his medicine and his supper, but Ann could not in good conscience leave Becky at the dog park alone. It would close soon, and then what would she do? After the park ranger came to lock the gate, they waited a little longer for Bruce in the parking lot. When he didn't show, they piled all three huskies into the back of Ann's car. Choco sat happily in the front seat on Becky's lap, attempting to lick her face. From the back, Ruger became territorial about Becky and showed his teeth at the little dog, but neither Ann nor Becky noticed. They talked about nothing in particular as they drove through town. They noted the ice cream shop they both loved. The Italian restaurant that had sadly shut down. Soon they were in Becky's gravel driveway. Becky unbuckled her seat belt and put her hand on the door handle.

"Do you have a key? Is your mom home?" Ann asked.

Becky turned, looked Ann in the eye, and deadpanned, "I have a key, yes, and my mom is dead."

The "mom is dead" thing usually caused a jolt in people. It stopped them in their tracks. Becky felt powerful when she said it. A "fuck you" to the world.

Ann met Becky's eyes, unflinching. She paused for a moment and said, "My *son* is dead."

Becky felt the jolt boomerang back. She hadn't realized Ann's son had died when she'd talked about him previously.

For Ann, it was the first time she'd ever said those words so bluntly.

The two stared at each other for a long moment.

Ann cleared her throat and adjusted her posture. "My son died six months ago in a car accident. He was in his first year of college and was home for Thanksgiving break."

Becky let that hang in the air for several moments, then said, "My mom died a little over a year ago. I had just decided to tell a judge I wanted to live with her instead of my dad. A car accident for her, also."

Becky bit her lower lip.

"Oh, Becky," Ann said.

In her crushing grief, it hadn't occurred to Ann that others were going through the same thing. She'd felt so alone. It hadn't occurred to her that *kids* were going through this kind of pain, often with no real support. She'd seen Becky's father, and he seemed like a real piece of work.

Ann reached out her arms, and the hardened Becky folded into them. The feeling of a woman holding her, of being *mothered,* soothed the deepest, most lonely ache in Becky's heart. She began to sob, and it felt good to cry. Ann held Becky for a long time, allowing her own tears to fall as well.

Finally, Choco wiggled in between them and began licking the tears off their faces, and this made them laugh. They had forgotten the dogs were even in the car.

Becky suddenly pulled back, remembering she had a guard to keep up, and said, "How are there so many car accidents? Why *the fuck* can't anyone drive?"

A pause, and then Ann began laughing, and Becky laughed too. More tears of sorrow and laughter ran down their cheeks.

"You have mascara running down your eyes," Becky said, gasping for breath.

"So do you," Ann replied. "You look like Alice Cooper."

"Who's she?" Becky asked, causing Ann to cackle, which only made Becky laugh more too.

Choco jumped back and forth from Becky's lap to Ann's. He had no idea what was going on. Ruger snarled at Choco, but Ann and Becky were laughing so hard, they didn't notice.

"Thanks for the ride. I should probably go inside. The dogs will be hungry," Becky said.

"I'm glad I brought you home today, Becky," Ann said.

"Same," Becky said.

She got out of the car. Becky started to walk away but then turned back. Ann rolled down her window. "Did you forget something?"

"How old was Liam?"

"He was just 18. Not much older than you."

Becky said, "My mom's name was Katie. She was 32."

Ann reached out her hand, and Becky squeezed it.

Driving away from the house, Ann started down the highway. Rounding a curve, she was met by the final hurrah of a beautiful pink-and-orange sunset.

Ann pulled over on the shoulder and stopped to watch it, thinking of Liam. He would have loved it. Or rather, he would have loved how *she* loved it. Sunsets were *her* thing. After he left for college, he'd sometimes text her sunset pictures from wherever he was, a way to tell her he was thinking about her, and that he loved her.

Ann thought about Becky the rest of the way home. She wondered what her mother Katie had been like.

Bruce pulled up to the dog park after dark, drunk. He got out of the truck and walked to the gates, rattled them, but they were locked. He peered in through the fence. He drove around the park looking for Becky, but she was nowhere to be found. Bruce figured Nancy probably gave her a ride home, and that was fine. Becky needed to be taught a lesson, he reasoned. She couldn't expect him to be at her beck and call after she'd talked back to him. She was always sassing him about something these days.

Puffed up with self-righteousness, he drove slowly through the parking lot. Rolling down his window, he tossed out a beer bottle, causing it to shatter on the pavement. He smiled, then tossed another one, enjoying the sound of breaking glass.

Wayne had been out taking a late evening walk through the park with Roach and Thor. He heard the glass shatter and watched Bruce's truck swerve all over the road as it headed out of Lake Woof.

One of these days, that motherfucker's going to kill someone, he thought, shaking his head.

CHAPTER 22

Blood

Nancy furrowed her brow. "Hey, Tommy, it looks like Rocky's paw is bleeding. He must have stepped in some of that broken glass in the parking lot on the way in."

Tommy's eyes widened. He looked at Rocky, noted the bloody paw prints on the concrete floor of the gazebo, and staggered back, grasping the bench as he sat down. Quickly putting his head between his legs, he moaned, "Oh no!"

Nancy said, "Just grab him and take a look at it. Maybe it's nothing, but that's kind of a lot of blood."

"A *lot* of blood?" Tommy pulled his shirt up to cover his eyes. He pulled it down for a second, glanced at his dog, and asked, "Can someone else look? Please! I'm not good with blood."

Ann crouched down and took hold of Rocky's paw. "He doesn't seem to be in much distress," she said reassuringly.

Tommy, his head turned away, said, "It'll be okay, Rock. Ann says you're alright."

Choco came over to Tommy and began licking his face.

"Not now, Choco." He shooed him off and put his head back between his legs.

Trish moved closer to Tommy and placed her hand gently on his back for support, eager for an excuse to touch him.

Tommy turned his head and looked up at her from between his knees, gratitude in his eyes.

"It looks like a piece of glass is stuck between his paw pads," Ann said.

"Oh God," Tommy wailed. "Oh no!"

Ann and Nancy shared a glance. Ann smiled.

Nancy rolled her eyes. "Who's a drama queen?" she laughed.

"I think I can get it out," Ann said, her eyes squinting for a better view of Rocky's paw. "I don't have my glasses on," she said.

Tommy said, "Sometimes I faint."

"Well, then lie down on the bench, Tommy. We don't need to be taking you to the ER today if you fall and bust your head," Nancy commanded.

Tommy swung his legs onto the bench, laying the back of his head down as Gretchen walked toward them to see what the commotion was about.

Rocky yelped, and Ann said, "He won't let me hold onto his paw long enough to get it out. He keeps pulling away."

Gretchen said, "We should take him to the vet."

Ann said, "Yes, but he shouldn't continue to walk on it, should he? The piece of glass is right there. It would be so easy to get out if he would hold still. I wish I had some tweezers. Can you help me?"

Tommy lay on the bench, his right forearm draped over his eyes.

"So, there was this time when I was a freshman in college. Did I tell you I went to college? I did one-and-a-half semesters before they kicked me out. Academic suspension or some nonsense. College wasn't for me. Anyway, I met this girl—real cute. Also a freshman, and she comes back to my room. I have barely had sex with anyone at that point. I'm 18, skinny, but she was cute, and she agreed to come back, and, well, we drank some hard cider, and this led to that, if ya know what I mean. It wasn't my first time, but pretty close to it. We were both shy and kept the lights off. But then we got into it."

Nancy asked, "Why are you telling us this Tommy?"

Gretchen added, "Yeah, what is your point?"

Tommy lifted his head and turned to them. "There *is* a point, and I am getting to it." He glanced at the blood on the concrete and quickly put his head back down, covering his eyes with his forearm once again before continuing.

"So, as I was saying, we were having a good time in my dorm room. My roommate was away. We were young and wild and free."

"I thought you were shy?" Gretchen said.

"We were *shy*, and then we got *less shy*," Tommy said.

Rocky yelped and pulled his paw away yet again. Choco came over and tried to put his nose in, but Ann shooed him away.

"I almost had it," she said, grabbing again for a hold on Rocky's foot.

"Tommy, your point?" Nancy asked.

"Well, the *point* is this. We get done doing what we were doing, and eventually, one of us flicks on the light, and it is a fucking blood bath. It looks like someone was murdered. The sheets, covered in blood. My fucking pillow? Blood."

Ann and Gretchen stopped to look at Tommy for a second. "Oh my God," said Ann. "What happened?"

"She got her period, that's what happened. All over my bed, right through to the mattress. She didn't know it was coming. It's as if I kinda—*knocked it* out of her." He smiled, a hint of pride in his face.

The women started to laugh.

"That's not the worst part," Tommy told them. "I stood up," he continued, "and that's when I noticed there was a goddamn bloody handprint on the wall next to the bed. Like an honest-to-God crime scene."

The ladies were roaring now.

"And, you know, I wasn't good with blood to begin with. I've always been queasy. Cried my ass off as a kid if I needed shots and fainted one time when I had to get a blood draw. Anyway, I look and see my bed and the bloody handprint, and I pass out cold. Hit my head on the dresser."

He sat up on one elbow and lifted his hair with the other hand, revealing a scar at the hairline. "I needed seven stitches for that."

He laid his head back down on the bench and continued, "So this chick thinks I had a seizure or something, and she calls 911. And as I'm coming to, firemen come busting into the room. They're looking around and see all the blood, and then the police come. She's already thrown some clothes on by this time, but I'm still, like, butt naked."

"It's 'buck naked,' Tommy," Gretchen corrected him.

"Whatever," Tommy said. "I'm naked, and the police fly in the door, and they have their guns pointed at me. They think someone got raped or killed, and I'm still kinda out of it. The girl is trying to tell them nothing bad happened, and I'm, like, what the fuck is going on?"

"Only you, Tommy," Nancy said, laughing so hard she had to wipe tears from the corner of her eye.

"We both got questioned by the police, and I had to get stitches in my head, which was another nightmare. The whole dorm knew all about it. It was just a horrible day in the life of Tommy."

He paused for dramatic effect.

"So, you know, I don't like blood. *That* was my point."

Ann finally succeeded in getting the shard of glass out of Rocky's foot. Gretchen ran the paw under cold water in the doggie shower hose and wrapped it in a clean bandana she had in her car. Trish offered to take Rocky to the vet so Tommy wouldn't have to deal with it all. Tommy was more than happy to take her up on it.

Hours later, when Trish dropped Rocky off at Tommy's apartment, it was past dinnertime, and he invited her in.

"Hey, are you hungry?" he asked.

"Starving," she said.

Tommy ordered them a pizza. As he hung up the phone, he glanced at Trish and paused. If he wasn't mistaken, she was looking at him a *certain kind of way.*

He smiled at her, raised his eyebrow, assessing the situation. She smiled back, then looked down at the floor.

"Trish, come here," he said, opening his arms wide, and pulling her into a hug. Her hair smelled like flowers.

"Thanks for taking care of Rocky today." He kissed the top of her head, sending chills down Trish's whole body.

She pulled back to look at his face. "You're welcome." She smiled.

She sure is pretty, he thought.

They each held the other's gaze, hovering in that moment just before. Electricity zipped back and forth between them.

Tommy leaned in to kiss her, and they made out until the pizza arrived.

CHAPTER 23

Lunch with Evan

Becky had been sitting in her bedroom, feeling bad about Rocky's hurt paw. At the dog park yesterday, Nancy told her what happened, saying, "Some idiot dropped glass beer bottles in the parking lot, and didn't bother to clean them up."

Becky suspected correctly it had been Bruce but didn't say so. For as long as Becky remembered, he loved to toss glass bottles out his window while driving. The sound of them breaking gave him some kind of thrill. He was so embarrassing to her.

Her phone beeped, and she was surprised when a text from Katie's husband Evan came through. She hadn't hugged her little brothers since Katie's funeral.

It had been a small funeral for Katie. Her parents, and some friends from high school. Evan and his family were there. Becky stood alone, in shock, shrugging off the hugs and pats and pity being rained down upon her. She stood numb as her mother's casket was lowered into the ground.

Bruce hid in the cemetery, watching. Disbelieving! Hating Katie had been his purpose for so long; he didn't know what he was feeling. What was it, joy? No. Grief? Not exactly. He knew he'd never really loved her. Was it gratitude for the gift she had given him, in Becky? No, he wasn't going there. Guilt? He shook off the notion. Fuck that. I didn't do anything wrong; she left me, he reasoned. He walked to his truck, which he'd parked on the other side of the cemetery, and left out a back exit so no one would see him.

Becky resented Evan for taking her mother away from her when she was little, but she did want to see Joey and Jack. Evan had tried to schedule visits for Becky and the boys previously, but Bruce had always shut him down. Katie's parents gave up trying to get Bruce to let Becky come to Florida, and had offered to fly up to visit her, but Bruce always had an excuse as to why it wasn't a good time. Finally, Katie's parents gifted Becky with a cell phone and took over the payment plan so Bruce couldn't argue. They at least could text and call her occasionally, but the relationship was strained and awkward. Becky felt she hardly knew them. Even though she resented Evan, he was one of the first people she texted when she got her new cell phone. She wanted the boys to have her phone number.

Now, Evan's text read, "We're going to be in Haberland City this weekend. Would you meet us for lunch? The boys would love to see you. We all miss you."

This time, Becky didn't ask for permission. On Saturday, she got Ann to give her a ride downtown. Bruce had been out drinking the night before and wasn't even awake when she left at 11 a.m. It felt so good to see her brothers again. Each one chattered away at her, competing for her attention, and she loved it. They got burgers and milkshakes and walked around a local park.

Evan took their picture on a bridge overlooking the lake and texted it to Becky's new phone. It meant the world to her to have that photo.

When Evan dropped her home, Becky breathed a sigh of relief when Bruce's truck wasn't in the driveway. She would have been in so much trouble if he found out she was with Evan and hadn't told him.

"Hang on a second," Evan said, hopping out of the car and taking a box out of the trunk.

Smiling at Becky, he handed it to her. "These are some of your mother's things. I know she'd want you to have them."

"Thank you," Becky said. Putting the box down, she hugged him hard. She didn't know what was in the box, but she had nothing of Katie's in her possession, and her heart filled with gratitude. Becky gave each of her brothers a long hug, and then they were gone again.

In her bedroom, she locked the door and opened the box. There was a scarf, several journals, and a pom-pom from when Katie had been a cheerleader. Becky took the pom-pom out and shook it in the air. She imagined Katie in high school, a cute young blond girl in a cheer uniform, one hand raised, shaking the very pom-pom Becky held in her hand. As a rule, Becky didn't like cheerleaders. She didn't care for anyone that was so happy the way cheerleaders always seemed to be for no reason, but she did not begrudge her own mother for being young and joyful once upon a time. There were some programs from school plays Katie had been in. Becky opened the program for the Haberland City Senior High School production of *Oliver*. Katie had been one of the orphans, part of the ensemble. Cool. Becky had never known that.

She counted seven numbered journals. Opening the first one, she gasped at her mother's perfect cursive. A chill went down her spine. Just then, Becky heard the wheels of Bruce's truck crunching the gravel driveway outside. She tucked the box deep under her bed.

CHAPTER 24

Katie Speaks

Bruce and I met in high school. I was a cheerleader. He was the star quarterback. Everyone thought we were the perfect couple. Here's the thing I think about all the time; I married him because I wanted to. The whole thing is my fault. I was never good at school, so getting married was an excuse not to go to college. I was in love with who I made him out to be in my mind, which was completely different than who Bruce actually was.

My parents thought we were too young to get married. They didn't hate him, but barely knew him because he rarely talked in their presence. They chalked it up to shyness.

The day we graduated high school, Bruce's dad kicked him out of the house. After that, he'd been living on his own for almost a year, and though he was in no hurry to get married, he was more than happy to have someone to split the bills with. I told Bruce I'd only move in with him if we tied the knot.

After I finally wore them down, my parents gave us their blessing and a nice down payment for the little house we purchased. My dad retired, and they moved to Florida a year after Becky was born. It had been their lifelong dream, and my decision to get married wasn't going to stop them. They made that clear. I had visions of us visiting them every year, taking Becky to play in the ocean. They didn't know the reality of what soon enough was going on for me, and I was too embarrassed to tell them. I'd been so hardheaded about getting married and didn't want to admit I'd been wrong.

Looking back, I'm not sure Bruce ever really loved me. I don't know if he's capable of loving anyone. He is obsessed with our daughter, but I wouldn't call that love. Becky has always been like another sports trophy for him.

When she was born, after I'd labored for 26 hours, the nurses swaddled her up and handed her to Bruce to present to me. On the way across the room, he stuck his index finger into her mouth. He stood beside my bed, not giving her to me.

I said, "Bruce, please give me my baby."

"She's my baby too, Katie," he said, without taking his eyes off her.

"Of course she is, Bruce, but c'mon, what are you doing?"

Gazing at Becky, his finger in her mouth, he said, "I just want to make sure I'm the first one she bonds with."

It was the first time I felt hate for him. He had to get right in there between us from day one. Finally, he left to celebrate her arrival with some of his football friends, and it was just me and her. It was the best moment of my life. I marveled at her thick dark hair. Her little squeaks. Her big dark eyes. The way she smelled.

Reading this, a tension in Becky's shoulders released. Of course, she couldn't remember the day she was born, but it *felt* like a memory, a visceral feeling of being held, and of being loved by her mother.

Returning to Katie's words in her own hand proved addictive. The journals went from high school, right up to the very day she died. Becky started by jumping back and forth but had now gone back and was rereading them in chronological order in short intervals behind Bruce's back. She was very careful. Becky didn't want Bruce's eyeballs on her mother's innermost thoughts and feelings. He didn't deserve them.

It started with him throwing things. He sent a vase my grandmother gave me sailing past my head crashing into the wall, this over a minor argument. Then, he shoved me a few times. But he only hit me that one time. We were fighting. I'd wanted to get Becky a puppy for her second birthday, and he said no.

I admit—I didn't let it go. I pressed him. I'd grown up with a Labrador retriever and wanted Becky to have the same experience because dogs are the most wonderful companions.

His response was to pin me to the wall, choking me with one hand and hitting me across the face with the other, twice.

Becky's blood went cold reading the entry. She remembered Bruce pinning her to the wall by her throat when she'd sassed him a few months back. At the time, he'd raised his hand and said, "You're just like your mother," before letting her go.

My parents always taught me if a man ever hits you, don't wait around for it to happen again. After I left him, he got Becky that first puppy, just to spite me. And he named it after his gun, which he knew I would hate. The gun he kept always made me nervous. You should have seen his smirk when he told me about Beretta, the first little husky pup.

For a few years we shared custody of Becky 50-50, and I ached for her when Bruce had her. It was as if I couldn't breathe until she was back with me each time. Bruce was a jerk to me, but I didn't think he'd ever hurt her.

Then, I met Evan. He was everything Bruce wasn't. Kind. Caring. Gentle. He treated Becky as if she were his own child. We got married and had our two little boys. Becky loved her baby brothers. I finally had everything I'd ever wanted, and Bruce couldn't stand that I was happy.

When Becky was six, she started becoming weird about her body. One day, she'd been doing a summersault in the living room, and I patted her on the bottom as I passed by. She pivoted. "Don't touch my privates. Daddy says no one is allowed to touch my privates."

Fear ripped through me in that moment as Becky glared at me. What the hell?

"Of course not, Becky. I guess I'm just used to you being a little kid, but I will not pat you on the bottom again if it makes you uncomfortable."

She folded her arms and looked at me suspiciously.

My intuition was on full alert, but I let it go. There would be no point talking to Bruce about it.

And then she walked in on us in the shower. The kids were watching TV. I thought I'd locked the door. Suddenly, Becky pulled the shower curtain open and caught us having sex. Evan tried to hide himself by turning to the wall, but Becky had already seen his penis. She recoiled back, her mouth open wide in shock.

I snapped the shower curtain shut and said, "What do you need, Becky?"

"I wanted to know if we can have a Pop-Tart?" she asked.

Evan and I locked eyes. He laughed nervously, covering his mouth with his hand.

"Sure, sweetie, that's fine," I said.

"Oh my God," I mouthed to Evan.

She left the bathroom and never said another thing about it. I hoped she hadn't seen much, and I didn't want to embarrass her. I didn't handle it well, not talking to her about it. I shouldn't have avoided it.

Reading the next entry, Becky noticed Katie's handwriting change from loopy cursive to frantic hard edges.

The letter from Bruce's attorney says he's filing for full custody.

I went to his house (the one my parents helped us buy, but somehow, he got to keep) and asked him what his problem was. That was the night he threatened to report Evan for sexual abuse.

"He exposed himself to our daughter," he said.

"Bruce, she walked in on us in the shower. It wasn't on purpose."

"Oh, I am well aware, Katie, that our daughter saw his giant dick while you were in the shower with him," he said.

"Bruce! It was an accident."

"Tell it to the judge, Katie, but I am fully confident I can get Becky to say you've been touching her privates and that the two of you have been having sex in front of her."

My head was spinning. He'd been grooming Becky to accuse us.

"It sure would be awful to have your husband listed as a sex offender, wouldn't it? Maybe you, too. I researched, and if he's found guilty, they will definitely give me full custody, and maybe even take Becky's half-brothers from you as well for something like this."

Bruce had forever corrected Becky. "Half-brothers," he would say, whenever she spoke of Joey and Jack as her brothers.

I couldn't bear telling Evan what Bruce was accusing him of. This was my fault for being stupid enough to marry him in the first place. I tried to research my rights online but was so overwhelmed. The letters flickered and jumped all over the pages in every article I pulled up. I called several attorneys, and they were so expensive. We could never afford them.

Evan was getting fed up with me. I was doing the bare minimum taking care of the boys and the house. I could hardly function. In just two months, I lost 14 pounds worrying about it. I started to keep a bottle of gin hidden in the garage. At night after Evan was asleep, I'd go out and drink to calm my nerves.

One night, I snuck out and drove to Bruce's house at 3 a.m. I knocked on his door and am not ashamed to say I got on my knees and begged him not to do this.

"Bruce, you know we are not abusing Becky. Why are you doing this?" I cried. "What did I ever do to make you hate me so much?"

He looked down at me with disgust. You know what he said to me, the mother of his child?

"All's fair in love and war."

He called me pathetic. He said he would destroy me.

And he did.

I had to choose between giving him full custody of Becky, or risk losing all my children.

After signing the forms, I ran to the bathroom and threw up. For over a year, I did the bare minimum for the boys and otherwise lay in bed in the dark, only pulling myself together for my visits with Becky. I only got to see her every other weekend, and I needed those visits to be happy for her sake.

Becky had never known Katie to be depressed. She thought her mother and Evan and her brothers were living it up, without her. Rage ripped through Becky as she read the entry. She stood with her hands in fists, shallow breaths, feet glued to the floor, afraid she would tear the whole house down if she dared move. Finally, after a long moment, Becky put her hands over her mouth, and began to cry. "Oh, Mommy."

A year after I gave him custody of Becky, we moved four hours away to Charleston. Evan had received a good job offer there. I could only see her every other weekend anyway.

I continued to put on a happy face for Becky and drove the four hours to see her twice a month but became so depressed my marriage fell apart. Our boys barely saw me get up off the couch. I rarely brought Evan or the boys with me to see Becky because I had a primal need to have her all to myself. Joey and Jack missed their sister, and they missed having a mother that was engaged. They resented how I left them every other weekend to see their sister. Evan missed me too, but I couldn't get it together. I ached for Becky every minute I wasn't with her. Our family was completely torn apart.

Meanwhile, Bruce convinced Becky I left her because of Evan. That it was his fault. That he didn't want her, and that I bent to his wishes. Nothing could have been further from the truth. Evan had always adored Becky and treated her as if she were his own daughter. Our lives would have been better in every way had Becky been with us.

Reading this, Becky felt shame for hating Evan all these years, and for blaming him. All the anger she'd felt for him instantly shifted toward Bruce.

Becky is 13 now. I finally asked her today if she might want to live with us. She's old enough to speak to a judge herself. She said she would think about it. I am hopeful I can make things right with her. I pray I can make it up to her. One day I will tell her everything. I will beg her to forgive me. I should have asked for help. Giving up custody of her was so stupid. I am so ashamed I signed those papers.

It was Katie's last entry. Becky held the journal to her chest while tears streamed down her face. It was all Bruce's fault, but Katie wanted to apologize.

White-hot hate for her father settled in the pit of Becky's belly.

She went into the bathroom and steadied herself, holding onto the cold sink. Her hands were shaking. She looked in the mirror.

After her mother moved away, Becky began observing the well-mothered girls in her classes, noting the signs. Outfits with matching shoes. Ponytails and braids neatly done. Notes left lovingly in lunch boxes. Girls who were headed to ballet class and piano lessons after school. Playdates between girls whose moms were friends. She had longed for all of it.

By sixth grade, she convinced herself she hated these girls. She would glare at them all day at school, pushing them away from her. Then, at night, alone in her room, she'd wonder why they didn't like her. She wondered why they didn't invite her to their slumber parties. She wondered what about her was so unlovable, so bad, her own mother would leave her behind.

When she'd told people at Lake Woof her mother died, she got sympathy, but Becky refrained from telling them the part that had caused her deep shame. She never mentioned how her mother abandoned her, years before her actual death.

Now, staring into her own eyes, she saw a girl whose mother *had* loved her, and had *never* wanted to leave her. Becky swallowed hard. She stood taller.

This changed everything.

In the weeks after Becky read Katie's journals, memories flooded in. She remembered how Evan had given both Katie and Becky flowers the day they got married. She remembered they'd worn matching white dresses, and then went to brunch at a fancy restaurant after leaving the courthouse.

She remembered when Joey was born. Then Jack less than a year later. How much fun she had helping her mommy take care of her baby brothers!

She remembered eating pizza almost every week with her family at the Italian restaurant downtown.

She remembered Evan reading bedtime stories to her and the boys as they fell asleep.

She remembered sneaking out of her bedroom and watching Katie and Evan slow dance in the kitchen, long after she was supposed to be asleep.

Once, Becky woke up scared from a bad dream, and Katie comforted her and moved her mattress into Joey and Jack's room. Becky slept in there almost every night after that.

Becky remembered her sixth birthday party. She could almost taste the chocolate cake Katie made for her. Evan had rented a bouncy castle. Becky remembered running around with her brothers, shrieking with laughter. She remembered lightness. She remembered being loved. A love so bright she'd had to block it from her memory until now in order to survive its loss. As Becky remembered that love, hate for Bruce grew in equal measure. She could barely stand the sight of him.

CHAPTER 25

Everything Is Not
Okay at Home

Her whole life, despite everything, Becky had loved Bruce. When
she was little, she adored him. Then, later, he was the parent that
hadn't left, so she forgave all his embarrassing bullshit. She forgave
him for talking bad about her mother and Evan and her brothers.
Becky forgave him for treating the waitstaff terribly when they went
to restaurants, and for haggling with teenage cashiers to the point
of making them cry.

Becky had even forgiven him for treating her like a servant. For
only making what *he* liked to eat. For driving drunk with her in the
truck. For increasingly staying out at Malone's Tavern 'til 1 a.m. and
then stumbling in, waking her up on school nights. Becky forgave
him for having to listen to him puke when he drank too much.
For the smell of stale beer and cigarettes in their home. For being a
man and the only one she'd had to rely on when she'd gotten her
first period. Bruce brought home granny Depends undergarments
and not real pads and refused to go back to the store to exchange

them. It was humiliating to have to wear them. Becky forgave him for constantly leaving her at the dog park. She let all these things slide because he had *wanted* her. Despite everything, as he often reminded her, *he* was the only one she had. The one who stayed.

But it had been a lie.

Bruce kept her from Katie because he was a mean, vindictive, competitive asshole. And now Katie was dead, and Becky had been robbed of all that time with her.

Becky fantasized about killing Bruce. He loved his gun so much. Wouldn't that be a way for him to go?

Sometimes passing her in the hallway at home, Becky's glare was so icy it startled Bruce.

"I guess someone is on the rag," he'd say, before stepping out back with the dogs to smoke a cigarette, a new habit he'd picked up since spending more time at Malone's over the last year.

Becky's English teacher phoned Bruce. "Is everything okay at home? Becky isn't the same girl she's always been. She's sullen and not participating in class. Becky is one of my best students, but I had to give her a 40 on a paper this week. It is so unlike her to not even try."

Bruce clicked the phone off. He had never received a call from a teacher about Becky. *What the fuck was going on?*

She refused to talk to him.

When Bruce wasn't home, Becky found herself taking his gun out of the drawer in his bedside table. She'd load it and unload it, slamming her open palm into the chamber, the weight of the gun in her hand somehow soothing. She hadn't held the gun in almost a year. The day she beat him at target practice had ended their time in the cornfield.

Becky fantasized about shooting him in the head while he slept and would immediately shake off the image. One time she stood in the mirror and held the gun to her own head, then thought of Katie and dropped it to her side. She unloaded it and put it away.

Since reading Katie's journals, Becky had not been able to sleep. She couldn't eat. She lay in bed, wishing she could make up lost time with her mother, knowing it would never come.

Bruce had been keeping his distance, sensing he'd better give Becky a wide berth, but his patience was growing thin. He began circling back.

"You know, I am sick of stepping in dog shit in the yard," he said one day as she did the dishes after supper.

Becky shrugged her shoulders. She had no plans to do more chores. She already did practically everything around the house. She'd never been tasked with picking up dog poop other than at the dog park. They generally just left it to dissolve in the yard.

Ruger, perhaps picking up on the tension in the house, was proving to be a psycho more and more each day. The dog was jumpy and would nearly take off your hand if you reached for his food bowl. Ruger refused to come when he was called. He seemed to have no fear of punishment, even from Bruce, who wouldn't hesitate to kick him if he crossed him.

"So, I guess I have to spell it out for you, Becky. I need you to get a garbage bag and go outside and clean up the yard, *now*. I spent 20 minutes scraping shit off my work boots this morning and could smell it all day in my truck."

"I have homework to do," Becky answered as she scrubbed the last dish, prolonging it.

"Well then you better get out there and do it quick, before you get to that."

She dropped the cast iron pan in the sink, whipped the towel off the fridge door handle, and dramatically dried her hands.

"There it is," Bruce said, "that bitchy attitude. Just like your mother."

Becky turned and glared at him long and hard. Then, hands on hips, she smirked and said, "Thank you for the compliment," before storming out back, letting the screen door slam behind her.

Becky stayed outside for 30 minutes without picking up any dog poop, pacing and cursing him under her breath. Then, she went back into the house and marched into her bedroom, again letting the door slam behind her.

Becky's room was still filled with sorrowful self-portraits, but there were other sketches now crowding her walls. Unbeknownst to them, she'd done portraits of all the regulars at Lake Woof. She'd sketched every dog at least a dozen times, and their friendly faces filled her bedroom. Becky dreamed of the day she could go away to college and get away from Bruce. Three more years. But how would she get there? How would she pay for it? How would she survive that long? Bruce kept saying college was a dumb idea and would certainly be offering her no support. "Your mother never wanted to go to college. Do you somehow think you're *better* than her?" he asked recently when Becky brought it up.

Becky lay on her back, closed her eyes, and thought of Katie. Her throat tightened, and a tear trickled down from the outside corner of her eye, missing her ear and falling into her messy dark hair.

Later, at the dog park, Iris and Trish were walking laps and invited Becky to join them. They'd noticed her dad yelling at her before driving off in a huff, leaving her there by herself with the three dogs once again. They were leery of the younger husky, but

Ruger hadn't given Gigi any trouble lately, and had never bothered Buster.

Becky walked beside them, offering clipped answers to their questions.

"Did you and your dad get in a fight?"

"Yes."

"Do you fight a lot?"

"Always."

"Always," Iris said.

"You guys don't get along?"

"He's an asshole."

Trish and Iris shared a worried glance, silently concurring. They took turns putting their numbers into Becky's phone.

"Hey, if you ever need anything, call one of us, okay?" Trish said.

"Call us," Iris said, putting her hand on Becky's arm, making a rare moment of full eye contact.

Becky shrugged. "Thanks."

Nancy, Ann, and Shane had already given her their phone numbers. It was embarrassing how they were all concerned about her, and she'd rather die than call any of them, but it also felt kind of nice that they cared.

CHAPTER 26

Choco

It happened so fast.

Nancy and Ann enjoyed a nice afternoon in the gazebo with Iris, Trish, and Becky. Iris was debuting the new contact lenses Trish had encouraged her to try, and she was wearing makeup. The ladies were oohing and ahhing, and Iris blushed, enjoying the attention. Ann had Choco on his leash, ready to go, but then Tommy jogged up with Rocky and Buster.

He came dancing in and, after singing the Rocky theme song, kissed Trish on the cheek.

Ann chuckled and said, "See you tomorrow," to Nancy and the gang.

As she approached the gate with Choco, Ann stopped to fish in her bag for the car keys. Ruger came up behind them, and Choco's tail went deep between his legs.

In an instant, Ruger clamped down on either side of Choco's spine. He picked the little Dachshund up in the air and began thrashing him violently side to side. Choco let out a high-pitched, primal wail.

Noisy chaos erupted behind Ann as the others ran toward them trying to stop the attack. Ann turned to see Ruger trouncing Choco.

Becky, Nancy, and Trish were screaming. The rest of the dogs ran toward the commotion, and Gretchen's whistle stopped them in their tracks. Suddenly, she was bellowing, "BRUCE! GET YOUR FUCKING DOG!"

Iris wailed, covering her ears with her hands. She began shrieking and rocking. Shane ran from the other side of the park and put his arms around her, whispering, "You're okay. Iris, you're okay."

Bruce left Becky at the dog park by herself hours earlier but had just entered the parking lot to pick them up. He'd been getting out of the pickup when he heard Gretchen screaming at him. He ran in through the gate and saw Ruger with Choco in his mouth, shaking him back and forth. Bruce screamed, "DROP IT!" and kicked Ruger in the ribs. Ruger dropped him, and Choco lay on the ground shaking and gasping for breath, eyes wide. A pool of blood started to seep out from underneath him onto the concrete.

Bruce picked up Ruger and stomped out to his truck, flinging him into the cab. He shouted through the fence for Becky to get their other dogs. Becky gathered Beretta and Magnum and put them in the back of Bruce's truck. She shut the tailgate and headed back toward the dog park.

"Get in the truck, Becky."

"I want to make sure Choco's okay."

"Get in the fucking truck, Becky."

She walked away from him. "NO."

How *dare* she tell him no! Bruce wanted to slap her, but he could not go back into the enclosure right now. Not after what just happened. He'd be lucky if the police weren't on their way as it was, and honestly, he was a little tipsy. He needed to get out of there. He hit the steering wheel with his hands and screamed, "FUCK!" Becky had become just like her mother. A little bitch. He looked at Ruger and saw blood on his muzzle. "WHY THE FUCK DID YOU DO THAT?" he screamed. "WHAT THE FUCK IS WRONG WITH YOU?" Ruger pressed himself against the passenger side window, attempting to get as far away from Bruce as possible.

Bruce peeled out of the parking lot with the dogs.

When they got home, he pulled into the driveway, yanked Ruger out by his leash, and dragged him into the house. The other dogs followed. He kicked Ruger repeatedly, then began pacing the house.

"FUUUUUUUCK!" he screamed.

He couldn't take it. He left and went straight to the liquor store where he bought a bottle of whiskey and took a long draw to calm his nerves. Then, he got on the highway and drove fast.

Two minutes after Bruce left the park, a police car pulled into the lot. Gretchen had called 911.

Choco lay on his side, gasping. Ann knelt down next to him to see where he was hurt. As soon as she touched him, Choco clamped down on her hand, opened his mouth, and bit her hard, again. Nancy had been reaching toward Choco too and pulled her hands back quickly, just missing being bitten herself.

Becky took off her David Bowie shirt and wrapped it around Ann's wounds. She stood there in a sports bra and jeans, so skinny her ribs poked out. She had not been eating in the weeks since reading Katie's journals.

"I'm sorry. I'm so sorry," Becky cried to Ann.

"Oh, Choco," Ann wailed. "Choco!"

The police called an emergency veterinary ambulance. When it arrived, the technicians wore long thick gloves and put a wool blanket around Choco to prevent themselves from being bitten as they lifted him into the ambulance. Choco thrashed and snapped at them.

Shane gave Becky his jacket to wear.

Tommy sat on the bench, his head between his knees, moaning, "Oh God. Oh no. Oh, Choco. The blood!" Trish rubbed Tommy's back. Shane held Iris's hand.

Becky looked at Ann and said, "Ann, I'm so sorry."

Ann looked up through tears and sobbed, "It's not your fault."

Nancy went over and wrapped her arms around Becky. "Everyone knows it isn't *your* fault, kiddo. I'm going to have Tommy and Trish take you and Teddy to my place, and I'm gonna take Ann to the hospital to get her hand looked at."

Ann's hand required stitches in two places. Her fingers, swollen and purple, stuck out of her bandages. The nurse had given Ann a medication for anxiety prior to the stitches because she couldn't stop shaking and wailing. Nancy sat quietly beside her, holding space, waiting for the drug to take effect. After Ann had calmed down a bit, Nancy stepped into the hall and called the emergency animal hospital Choco had been taken to.

"He has severe internal injuries. We are doing everything we can to stabilize him. We will let you know."

They waited for Ann to be released from the ER.

Ann told Nancy the story she'd already heard several times but was happy to hear again. The day they got Choco, Liam had been speechless for a full 30 seconds before tenderly picking him up and whispering, "Hi, Buddy. Hi, Choco. You made it."

"He always knew in his heart Choco would one day arrive," Ann said.

She told Nancy how Choco would wait at the door for Liam when he wasn't home. How he slept in Liam's bed every night of his life. How Choco had too many nicknames to count.

Choco-lock-o.

Chock-full-o-nuts.

Chocomotive.

Count Chocula.

Choco Choco bo bock-o.

Sausage.

Davis (it took a few years for that one to be funny).

Brother.

Bruh.

Ann said, "Since Liam died, Choco has been a bridge to him, you know? If he doesn't make it, I'm afraid Liam will really be gone forever."

She began to sob again, and Nancy put her arms around her friend.

After the hospital, Ann and Nancy went to the emergency vet. It was almost 11:00 p.m., and they were both exhausted. Nancy's limp was worse than ever. Her whole body ached.

The young veterinarian noted Ann's hands, tilted her head, and made a pout with her mouth, shaking her head, then said, "Choco is stable right now."

Ann breathed a sigh of relief.

"But it isn't good," she continued. "He's got severe injuries to his internal organs. His back is broken. We can operate, but there is no guarantee he will survive the surgery. And even if he does, it will be a long painful recovery for him. He will most likely never walk again and would require a wheelchair device. He would need a lot of care and would likely always be in pain."

Ann felt her knees buckle, and the doctor helped Nancy assist her to a chair.

The veterinarian continued, "The kindest thing, and I know it is the hardest thing, but the *kindest* thing would be to put Choco down."

Ann sobbed. It was too much. This day was too much. This *life* was too much.

Nancy held Ann, rocking her like a baby.

Ann spoke through sobs, "I don't want him to suffer."

The vet said, "He's stable for the moment. You can come see him if you want to."

Ann and Nancy went into the OR. There was Choco. He lay on his side, with a tube down his throat. Machines were suctioning fluids out of his lungs. His normally soulful eyes were vacant. He had a large bandage wrapped around his entire torso. Blood seeped through the bandage, and a fist-sized stain was slowly expanding on the pad underneath him. Ann put her lips to his ear and felt the velvety softness.

"Choco. I am so sorry. You are the best boy, and you didn't deserve this. I know you didn't mean to bite me, Choco. I want you to know the day you arrived was not only the best day of Liam's life, but it was also the best day of mine. You made Liam the happiest boy in the world, and for that I am so grateful. Thank you for being here for me this last year. I've needed you, Choco. Thank you, Choco, best boy, ever."

Choco had been running the fence with Wayne's dogs just hours earlier. How was this possible? Liam had been joking with Ann 30 minutes before *his* accident. Ann wondered how those we loved could be taken from us so quickly, without warning. It was so cruel.

The vet popped her head in the door. Nancy waved her off.

Nancy's knees ached. She hoped Teddy was okay but knew Becky would take good care of him. *Oh, Becky.* She hoped Becky was okay. *That rat bastard father of hers,* she thought.

Ann's index finger stuck out of her bandage, and she stroked Choco's face with it. His eyebrows. His little stubby legs. His tail. She held one of his thick little paws in her other hand. She wanted to remember the feel of his fur. She ran her finger over the cowlick places where it appeared his seams had come together. She scratched behind his ears. He always loved that.

She told him she was sorry a hundred more times.

She thanked him a hundred more times for all the joy he had brought to Liam, and to her. And the next time the doctor popped her head in, Ann looked up and nodded.

The doctor had the syringe already drawn up. Ann held Choco's paw, her lips whispering love into his ear, and Nancy placed her hand on Ann's back. The doctor pushed the plunger on the syringe slowly forward, and in seconds, Choco, Mayor of Lake Woof, was gone.

At Nancy's house, Teddy greeted them at the door.

Ann winced in pain as she set her purse on the floor. Nancy limped through the living room and into the kitchen.

Becky had left a note. "Teddy has been fed. I asked Tommy to take me home. Tell Ann I'm so sorry."

Nancy took out the bottle of pain pills they'd given Ann at the ER. She'd been smart enough to ask the nurse to open the childproof container before they left. They'd been prescribed for Ann, but Nancy took one too. She went out on the back porch to have a cigarette, and when she came back in, Ann was asleep on the sofa.

She covered her friend with a blanket and said, "C'mon, Ted, let's get some rest."

CHAPTER 27

Nancy

Nancy couldn't believe the day had turned into such a shit show, and she knew of shit shows. She'd grown up in a tight-knit community in the Bronx. Everyone knew everyone. Everyone else's mother or grandmother would hang their heads out the window and yell at you if you needed it. No one was shy about it.

She'd known her husband Anthony since they were kids. They started dating in high school and got married shortly after. It's what you did. Anthony was a good-looking guy, and while she wasn't magazine-cover beautiful, she was big-hipped and broad when skinny was in, she was popular because she was funny, and she was beautiful in an unconventional way. She had big, dark eyes and a smile that lit up a room. Nancy was a good person, always there for her family and friends. Anthony loved her. They'd been in love. His whole life she'd been making him laugh.

They weren't blessed with children, and that had caused her heartbreak early on, but she'd accepted it. Anthony had low motility, and he didn't want to adopt. They had an active life together. She worked as a receptionist at a national pet food chain, and every week, she played cards with the friends she'd known since kindergarten. They went to the same Catholic church as everyone else she knew. They loved going to Yankee games together. They went bowling every Saturday with her best friend Francesca and her husband, also named Anthony but who went by Tony. Her life might not have been super exciting, but what do you want? She was content.

There was passion in the early years and still plenty of laughter almost 30 years in, but eventually they felt more like siblings than lovers. After her rheumatoid arthritis developed, the pain in her joints kept her from being active. She gained weight. She took comfort in Anthony spooning her at night and fell asleep to the sound of his snoring. They seldom had sex anymore. *It is what it is*, she figured.

And then Anthony slept with Francesca.

"We didn't plan it!" he pleaded as Nancy began flinging his clothes into the one suitcase they shared.

"It just happened," Anthony said.

"Your dick just happened to accidentally slip into my best friend's hoo-ha? That's what you're tryin' to convince me? Like it was a fuckin' mishap?" Nancy turned to look him in the eye. He averted his gaze and stared at the floor.

"We never meant to hurt you," he muttered.

"Now, you look at me, Anthony, you fucking coward. I want you to see my eyes."

Anthony looked up to meet her glare.

"For two people who never meant to hurt me, you sure did the most hurtful thing you could possibly do to me, Anthony. It's humiliating. The whole town knew too, right?" she asked.

He hung his head in confirmation, and Nancy yanked a drawer of his clothes out of the dresser and dumped it.

"Ya know what? Fuck you, Anthony. And fuck her. But I don't even have to say that, right? Because that's what you've already been doing. Fucking. Right behind my back."

Pushing Anthony out of the apartment, the last thing she said to the love of her life was, "You're dead to me. You both are."

She slammed the door.

Walking over to the dresser, Nancy picked up a framed photo of their wedding day. Her hands shook as she held it. There they all were. Her and Anthony. Francesca, her maid of honor, and Tony. She and Anthony had been married just a few months ahead of them. She wondered if Tony knew yet. Nancy's tears dropped onto the glass in the frame. She fell to her knees and wept.

A few weeks later, Francesca and Anthony were already shacking up. Nancy could not face the neighborhood with them living together. She felt ugly. Frumpy. It made her crazy how everyone had known, but no one had mentioned anything to her. She decided to move away from all she knew and rented an apartment in Haberland City, SC, after briefly researching the best places in the US to retire. She didn't want Florida and was sick of winter snow. *Fuck New York.* She got a main-level one-story apartment and adopted a two-year old giant yellow lab from The Humane Society to keep her company.

Nancy continued her employment with the same company, working from home for a few years, and then her arthritis became worse.

At first, she would lie awake at night thinking about Anthony and Francesca, and sometimes still did. What were they doing? What were they wearing? They'd had so many good times together as couples. She and Anthony had often laughed until tears came as they settled into bed, reliving their nights out with Francesca and Tony. Did Anthony and Francesca feel guilty? Did he ever regret it? Did he think of her? Did he miss the curve of her hip as he spooned her from behind? "Snug as bugs in rugs," they used to say. She thought they'd been a perfect fit. The only thing that gave her solace was the fact that Francesca was not funny. She might have had a nice ass, but he couldn't possibly laugh with her.

Nancy named her new dog Teddy because he immediately insisted on sleeping in her bed and let her cuddle him like a teddy bear. Teddy didn't laugh at her jokes, but at least he'd been loyal.

In the mornings, she woke so stiff she had to take a cold bath just to be able to move. It was rough on her mentally, applying for disability payments. She only worked part-time now. Nancy went to the dog park each day because it wasn't fair to Teddy to be trapped inside, and it kept her social. She'd always been a people person. She enjoyed hanging out with Ann, and the younger kids. It kept her from losing her mind.

It wasn't such a bad life. No one was bothering her. Yes, there was pain, but who didn't have some kind of pain in their life?

In the evening, she watched her shows, and the Yankees of course, during baseball season. She bought a rotisserie chicken from Publix, and she and Teddy ate half. She saved the rest for the next day. She lit another cigarette.

Nancy sometimes checked in with her cousin Carrie back in the Bronx to get the gossip on the neighborhood. Sometimes she asked about Anthony. Sometimes she didn't.

Nancy patted Teddy's rump as the medication began to kick in. "It was a shit day, Ted."

Opening his eyes, he stared adoringly into hers, and sighed.

"Our boy Choco is gone," she told him.

A tear ran down Nancy's cheek. Teddy moved closer, licked the tear from her face. Turning over, he pressed his back into her, settling in. She draped her arm over his large frame, taking comfort from his warmth as she fell into a drug-induced slumber.

CHAPTER 28

Finger On the Trigger

Bruce's truck wasn't in the driveway when Tommy and Trish dropped Becky off at home. She ran into the house, and Beretta and Magnum excitedly greeted her. Ruger was hiding at the end of the hallway by the bedroom doors. He barely lifted his head; he was in pain from Bruce's beating.

Becky's pants were covered in blood from trying to help Ann. Her thoughts were of Choco, writhing on the concrete.

She looked at Ruger and hated him. His meanness. His pushiness. His out-of-control everything. He was a bully, just like Bruce. Ruger watched her but didn't move.

She flashed to her mother, on her knees, Bruce's cold face saying, "All's fair in love and war." Katie had written he'd shown no compassion at all.

Becky left Ruger where he was. She took a shower, changed her clothes, and waited to hear from Ann and Nancy.

She checked her phone every five minutes.

Around midnight, when Nancy's text came in telling her Choco had died, Becky felt shame and rage. She put the older dogs in Bruce's bedroom and grabbed the gun from his nightstand before closing the door.

Ruger got up gingerly from the floor. He sniffed under the bedroom door for the other dogs. Becky watched him as she loaded the gun.

Ruger scratched at the bedroom door, wanting to be with Beretta and Magnum.

"Ruger," she cried.

At the end of the hallway, at the sound of her calling his name, Ruger turned toward Becky.

"You can't go around hurting other peoples' pets," she said. Hands shaking, she aimed the gun at him. She put her finger on the trigger.

Ruger blinked. He limped a couple of steps toward her, then lay down again.

"You're never going to get better, and he's just going to keep beating you," she said.

"You're a *bully*," she shrieked. "You fucking killed *Choco!*"

Then, just as Bruce had taught her, she swallowed her tears, steadied herself, looked through the sight, and aimed the gun between Ruger's eyes. There was a long pause, but Becky couldn't make herself pull the trigger.

Crying, she dropped to her knees, setting the gun beside her on the floor.

Ruger tried to get up to come to her. He stood halfway, then fell. His body started to shake as if he were having a seizure. Becky ran to him, wrapping her arms around him. He shook violently for another moment, then was still. Becky felt a chill run through her body as Ruger's spirit lifted up and out. Beretta and Magnum barked wildly from inside Bruce's bedroom. Becky trembled, rocking Ruger's body like a baby. "I'm sorry, Ruger. I'm so sorry," she wailed.

Becky took a blanket off her bed, and wrapped Ruger in it. Then, she wrote a note and set it beside his body. She put the gun, Katie's journals, and a change of clothes in her backpack and took off on foot.

CHAPTER 29

The Note

Bruce drove for about an hour, then pulled off onto a country road before stopping the truck. The whole time he'd been thinking of Becky and how she'd refused to come with him when he left the dog park. How dare she defy him that way, and in front of so many people? He shook his head. After all he'd done for her! Being the parent with sole custody all these years! He turned the truck around and got back on the highway toward home. He'd deal with her when he got there.

Swigging from the bottle of whiskey he held in his hand, Bruce thought, *Things like this happen sometimes. Dogs fight. It's no one's fault. Ruger must have felt threatened.* That's what he'd tell the police if they came. It had happened out of the blue. No one saw it coming. Animals were wild at heart.

He felt a twinge of guilt for beating Ruger but pushed it aside. The dog needed to be taught not to attack other dogs. It had to be done. He might have gotten a bit out of control, kicking him like that, but how else would the dog learn?

Occasionally, Bruce gently swerved across the yellow lines, then yanked the wheel back to correct it. Yawning, he decided to train Ruger better. He wouldn't take him to the dog park for a long time. Maybe he'd only take one at a time, like that Amazon bitch Gretchen told him to do.

He thought again, *No, I'll take two dogs. Fuck her. She can't tell me what to do.*

Bruce pulled into the driveway and took three clumsy tries to get the key into the lock on the front door, given the whiskey's effect on his coordination.

Swiping the wall for the light switch, he missed, so he staggered down the hall in the dark. Bruce heard the dogs whining and crying behind his bedroom door and tripped over Ruger's body on the way into his bedroom. He broke his fall with his hands.

What the fuck? His head spun.

Standing up, he flicked on the light, and saw Ruger's body on the floor, wrapped in Becky's bedspread.

As he opened his bedroom door, the older dogs frantically bounded out. They'd shit all over his bedroom carpet.

For a moment, Bruce panicked. Where was Becky?

Then, he saw the note lying against Ruger's body.

"Fuck you, Bruce. For everything."

He stumbled into the bedroom and opened the drawer of the bedside table. His gun was missing. "Jesus, Becky," he said, assuming she'd shot Ruger and run off with his gun.

CHAPTER 30

A Knock on the Door

In the middle of the night, Ann was in a fetal position on Nancy's sofa. Her bandaged hand throbbed. Choco was gone. Liam was gone. In her half-lucid state, her suicide fantasy clicked into place once again. Ann dreamed of a lethal injection. Lying down in a meadow, and just letting go. She wondered again why euthanasia was allowed for dogs, but humans were forced to endure so much unbearable pain.

There was a knock at the door, but Ann ignored it.

The knocks became louder, and then she heard a wail. It sounded like a child, crying.

"Nancy! PLEASE OPEN THE DOOR! PLEASE!"

Becky?

Ann got up and walked toward the door. She heard Nancy stir in her bedroom. Anger flooded Ann's body, as she imagined Bruce standing behind Becky on the porch. She clumsily opened the door and saw Becky there, alone.

Becky was shaking. She looked so tiny. Her eyes were red and swollen, like Ann's. Her legs were stick-thin in her skinny jeans, and her collarbones stuck out. Nancy came out from her bedroom wearing a T-shirt, and boxer shorts.

Trembling, Becky looked at Nancy, then locked eyes with Ann and said, "I didn't shoot him. I didn't fucking shoot him," she repeated over and over.

Becky fell to her knees and brought her forehead to the floor. Her body shook as she wailed.

"Who didn't you shoot, Becky? What are you talking about?" Nancy shrieked.

"Ruger. He's dead. I thought about shooting him, after what he did to Choco, but I couldn't. I didn't. But he died anyway. My dad beat him, and now he's dead."

Nancy put her hands to her heart. "Oh, Becky. Jesus."

Becky lifted her head, glanced up through her bangs at Ann.

"I kept telling my dad not to take him to the dog park. He was getting more and more aggressive, but he wouldn't listen to me. I'm so sorry, Ann!"

Ann said, "Choco's death is not *your* fault, Becky. You are not responsible for your father's actions. I am not mad at *you*, and I will never hold anything your father does against *you*, okay?"

Ann held out her arms, and Becky fell into them. Nancy wrapped her arms around both, and all three wept.

Becky cried, "Oh, Choco, I'm so sorry."

Teddy came out and assessed the situation. He lay down on the floor in front of the sofa, resting his chin on Nancy's foot.

Nancy stroked Becky's hair and said, "It's okay, Becky. You're okay. It's all going to be alright."

CHAPTER 31

Looking for Becky

Midday, after he sobered up, after he put Ruger's body, still wrapped in Becky's blanket, in a black garbage bag and tossed it on the side of an old country road, Bruce set his sights on finding Becky. How dare she kill his dog? That dog cost $300. Not what you'd typically pay for a husky, but the breeder cut him a deal on account of Ruger's fucked-up teeth and "off" temperament. Anyway, he was going to see to it that Becky paid him back with her own money. She'd have to pick up odd jobs to earn it.

He would also inform her she'd be paying for replacing the carpet in the bedroom where the dogs had shit on the floor after being locked in there *by her*. What a piece of work she had become. And where the fuck was his gun? She'd better have it, or she'd be paying for that too. Becky was in so much trouble.

What had gotten into his daughter? Bruce shook his head, then rubbed his chin with his forefinger and thumb with one hand, steering the truck with the other.

Sure, she was upset about Ruger getting into a tussle with the little wiener dog, but dogs fought. What were you gonna do? Choco was probably fine. Everyone at the damn park, making a big deal of things, acting like his dogs were worse than anybody else's. Well, his dogs had just as much right to go to the city-owned dog park that he paid for with his damned taxes as everyone else's dogs did.

He knocked on Nancy's door.

Becky had gone to Ann's house earlier. She was not ready to see Bruce yet, and Ann said she had a guest room Becky could rest in.

It took Nancy a while to open the door, and when she did, Teddy stood behind her. He let out a soft growl, uncharacteristic of him.

"Hey, Nancy, do you know where Becky is?" Bruce asked, standing with his hip cocked to the side, eyes looking up over her right shoulder, impatiently.

Nancy blinked.

"When we tried to help Choco yesterday, he was in so much pain, he bit Ann's hand twice. We had to take her to the emergency room for stitches."

Bruce stepped back and let out a big sigh. "Shit—uh...is Becky here?"

Nancy stared him in the eye, letting him stew in discomfort for a long moment.

"Not a good look, Bruce, to leave your daughter at the scene of the crime, to face things herself."

Bruce said, "Now, Nancy, you know there was no actual crime committed, right? Dogs get in tussles all the time. My dog ain't the one that bit Ann."

Nancy shook her head.

"Bruce, Choco is *dead*. Ruger bit down into him and thrashed him so hard he broke his back. He sustained injuries the vet said he could never recover from. Ann's dog is dead. And Ann got the shit bit out of her. And you *knew* your dog had a problem, but you kept bringing him around. And you *knew* folks were leaving the park whenever you arrived, to avoid him. And now this whole mess. And it may not be a crime, in the legal sense of the word—or maybe it is; I don't know—but it is a crime in a *human* sense. Where is your compassion?"

Bruce dug in his heels.

"I didn't commit any crime, Nancy, but a crime was committed at my house, because I came home to find my dog shot dead, by my own daughter, who left a note saying she did it. And I want to know where she is."

"She isn't here, Bruce. And Becky would *never* hurt one of her dogs. She's not like you."

Bruce reeled back and said, "You don't know what the fuck you're talking about Nancy. And you'd best not be lying about her being here."

He turned and went quickly down the sidewalk.

"She is in a *shitload* of trouble," he yelled over his shoulder before slamming the door of his truck and peeling out of the driveway.

Nancy picked up her phone. "Ann, is Becky still with you? Don't drop her off at home right now. Bruce just came by here, and he is completely unhinged."

CHAPTER 32

The Standoff

Bruce returned home to see if Becky was there yet. She wasn't. After a while, he finally thought of Ann. Becky seemed to like that lady, the same way she liked Nancy. It made him uneasy, the way those two women took to his daughter. They talked with her like it was so easy, and she would laugh and talk with them too.

She *never* talked to him anymore.

He knew Ann lived in one of the historic houses downtown, the big ones with the wrap-around porches and whatnot. She was rich. He didn't feel too bad about Choco. *I mean, it was a shame, but sometimes dogs fight,* he reasoned. *They are stupid animals.* And it wasn't like that lady couldn't easily afford another wiener dog.

He walked up onto her porch and knocked hard on the door. Ann answered, leaving the chain lock in place, talking to Bruce through the small space in the open door. He tried not to look at her bandaged hand.

"Is Becky here?" he asked.

"Yes," Ann answered curtly.

"Can I come in?"

"No. You may not."

Bruce stood there, weighing his options. What he felt like doing was busting through the chain lock, marching into the house, and yanking Becky out by her hair. But he didn't exactly feel like being arrested.

"Well, Becky needs to come with me. *Now!*" he bellowed.

Ann filled with rage. "You're something else, aren't you? You come here yelling, after your dog kills my dog, and you don't even mention it, don't even apologize?"

"Look, lady. Dogs get in tussles. It happens. Maybe your little wiener dog set him off. It's not like I planned to have the dogs get in a fight, for fuck's sake. Circle of life and all that."

Steely, Ann said, "I don't know how someone who is such an asshole has a kid as great as Becky. She obviously takes after her late mother."

Bruce's eyes bulged.

"BECKY!" he yelled. "GET YOUR ASS OUT HERE RIGHT NOW!"

Becky came from around the corner. She heard what Ann said, and it filled her with strength.

"I'm not going home with you," she said.

"The hell you ain't!" Bruce shouted into the house.

He rattled the door, and Ann stopped him with a wrath and conviction that surprised them all. "Get back. And if you step onto my property again, I will have you arrested for trespassing! I mean it."

Bruce stood there, looking over Ann's shoulder at Becky, who stared him in the eye from across the room. He pointed at her. "You get your ass home by 3 p.m., or I will call the cops to have them come drag you out of here. You got it?"

Becky stood stone-faced, her insides trembling with rage. Tucking her hands into her pockets, she secretly gave him the finger with both hands.

Bruce turned and stomped back to his truck, slammed the door, and took off out the driveway.

At 3:30 p.m., Becky's phone blew up with 17 messages, all some version of, "GET YOUR ASS HOME NOW."

At 4 p.m., Bruce showed up at Ann's again. He knocked on the door, hard.

She kept the door shut this time, but opened the front window a crack and said, "Get off my property, Bruce. I have asked you to leave, and I will have you arrested if you don't get off my property this instant. I don't want you in my house, on my porch, or in my yard." Her voice was low, powerful, and dignified.

Bruce screamed, "Becky! Get the fuck out here. You are coming home *now!*"

There was a knock on the glass of an upstairs window. Bruce stepped off the porch to see Becky in the window, hands out of pockets, flipping him off, both hands. Meeting his gaze, she slowly shook her head no.

Bruce's eyes widened. He sucked in his breath. Sputtering, he got in his truck and peeled out of the driveway, headed home to think.

Back at his house, Bruce realized he'd forgotten to take Beretta and Magnum out before he left. They had shit all over the floor again.

He screamed, "GODDAMMIT!"

The dogs cowered in the corner as he cleaned it up.

Bruce paced around his foul-smelling home. He called Becky again and left a message. "I mean it, Becky. If you don't come home by 7 p.m., I am calling the cops to have *them* bring you home."

Bruce didn't know Ann had worked with the local police department for years as part of the Building Bridges team at the college. She'd already given the supervisor a call to see what their options were. She couldn't in good conscience send Becky home to Bruce right now with how ramped up he was. Ann felt Becky would truly be in danger but needed to know her rights.

Bruce showed up at 7 p.m. with the police whom he had called to the scene. Ann was relieved to see the supervisor had sent two officers she knew. One winked at her as he shook her hand to "introduce" himself.

Becky came to the living room as Bruce stood waiting in the middle of Ann's front yard.

They asked Becky if she was okay.

She said, "Yes."

They asked if she was safe.

She said, "Yes."

They told Becky her father wanted her to come home with him, and she replied, "I don't want to go home. I don't feel safe with my father right now."

The officer stepped back onto the porch and reminded Bruce that Ann told him he was not allowed on her property. He asked him to step off onto the sidewalk.

The officer told Bruce what Becky said and added, "I'm not going to drag her out of there if she says she doesn't feel safe. We can call Child Protective Services and let them sort this out if you like, or you can let her stay here a few more days and let it blow over. That's what usually happens in situations like this."

Bruce's arms were folded over his chest, and he shook his head.

"She's lying saying she doesn't feel safe with me. She's been with me all her life. I'm a single parent! I got custody of her when she was little. *I've* been the one taking care of her, *not* her mother."

The officer nodded. "That may or may not be true, but if it were me, I'd give her a little time rather than getting Child Protective Services involved."

Bruce stormed back to his truck and peeled out of the driveway.

He mulled over the officer's advice and decided to let Becky be for a couple of days, but knowing she was over there with Ann and Nancy rattled him. Lying in bed the next night, he began to feel a familiar panic, a trembling in his legs.

Bruce remembered walking by Antonio's pizza place on Main Street one day when Becky was six, before he'd been awarded full custody. He'd been headed to a bar downtown. Bruce had washed his car, cleaned the bathroom, tidied the house, just in case. He'd put on his best shirt, his best boots, and too much cologne.

He circled around the downtown area a few times and finally found a parking spot a few blocks away. Haberland City was always crowded on the weekend, but he was in a good mood and didn't mind the walk. He felt the freedom of a childless evening.

Rounding the corner, he caught sight of them in the restaurant window, and took it all in. Red checkered tablecloths. The baby in a highchair. The toddler in a booster seat. Becky smiled at Evan, and Bruce's heart sank. He stepped behind a pillar before they could notice him, not that they would have. They were all laughing and talking. The baby had tomato sauce all over his face. The waitress stood, hand on hip, relaxed. She said something, and they all laughed. Becky tipped her head back and smiled broadly. The slice of pizza she held, bigger than her head. The way Evan looked at Katie, and at Becky. It was clear—they were a family.

Bruce suddenly felt hot and sick. A burst of adrenaline made his legs shake. He started running, and by the time he got back to his truck, he was having trouble drawing breath. He thought he might be having a heart attack or a stroke. He moaned and thrashed, sure he was about to die. Bruce thought about calling 911, held the phone in his hand ready to do it, but felt embarrassed. All he could think of was Becky. He felt as if she were being ripped away from him, as if Katie and Evan were stealing her from him. Bruce had the sensation that Becky was falling into an abyss he'd never be able to pull her out of.

Twenty minutes later, he sat limp in his truck, hands on heart, as his body finally began to calm. His shirt was damp, his hair a mess. After a while, he put the truck in gear and drove home, shivering and alone.

Three days after his panic attack, Becky was back at his house. It was a normal day. As they watched TV that evening, snuggled up with Beretta, Bruce fished casually, floating out a question he'd asked before. It had always come up empty.

"Do your mother and Evan ever walk around naked? Have you ever seen Evan naked?"

That's when Becky told him about walking in on them in the shower.

CHAPTER 33

Becky's Plan

Ann, Becky, and Nancy weighed Becky's options. They couldn't figure out what to do. Finally, after months of no contact, Ann called her best friend Helen.

"I need you," Ann said.

"I've been waiting," Helen replied, adding, "I've got you."

Ann filled Helen in on the last several months, and on the current situation. After discussing it with Helen, Ann's police friends, and two social workers, they knew the only way to keep Becky out of Bruce's house was to file a case with Child Protective Services. They would keep it simple, so as not to get Becky thrown in juvie. They would not mention the gun she stole from her father. Becky had faith Bruce wouldn't mention it because he'd purchased it illegally, and charges could be pressed against him if a minor under his care had used it. She was certain he knew that much because he told her that all the time.

225

Bruce awoke to social workers knocking on his door, accompanied by a police officer. The dogs barked like crazy, the sun hurt his eyes, and he blinked. The CPS workers could smell booze from the night before seeping off him, and the place reeked of dog feces. They informed him a case had been filed against him.

"What the fuck are you talking about?" Bruce said.

One of the social workers explained that Becky had alerted Child Protective Services herself. "She said she doesn't feel safe with you. She accuses you of putting her in harm's way."

"That's a lie," Bruce hissed.

The social worker continued, "Becky says you left her at the dog park with no way to get home after your dog mauled another dog. She says you sometimes don't come home at night. She says you drive drunk with her in the car. Your daughter says you are emotionally abusive to her and physically abusive to your dogs."

"I'm not abusive to the dogs. The puppy just needs discipline because he's an asshole. Or—he *was* an asshole," Bruce said.

The social worker and police officer looked at Bruce questioningly.

"I didn't kill him," he said.

"What *did* kill the dog, Mr. Owen?" asked the officer.

Bruce still thought Becky shot Ruger, but he couldn't tell the cops that. They'd want to see his gun, and he had no idea what she'd done with it. They would really take Becky away if they knew he let her use it and didn't lock it up.

"I had him put down, okay?" Bruce said.

"Because of the fight at the dog park?" the social worker asked.

"Yeah," Bruce said, folding his arms over his chest. "Because of that whole situation."

Now that there was an open case with CPS, Bruce was advised by the social worker involved to leave Becky alone until it was sorted out, but he showed up with the police at Ann's house three more times that week. Each time, he paced the sidewalk, ranting. Bruce didn't make the connection that his angry blather made it clearer to the police why Becky didn't feel safe with him.

Each time, the police went through the motions, telling Becky that Bruce wanted her home. Each time, Becky repeated she didn't feel safe, and they refused to force the issue.

Becky had been at Ann's house for a week. That evening, Ann, Nancy, and Becky sat on the big wraparound porch talking, with Teddy snoozing at their feet. Ann said, "While I would love to have you stay with me, Becky, he's likely not going to let you live here forever. I'm not sure the CPS case is strong enough to have you removed from the home."

Becky's eyes welled up, and she bit her lip.

"What is it, Becky? What's wrong?" Nancy asked. "I mean, I know the situation is currently shit."

Becky began to sob and told them everything. She shared what she read in her mother's journals. She told them how Bruce had kept her from Katie all those years, and now she would never see her again. How he'd convinced her as a child that Katie hadn't wanted her, but now she knew it hadn't been true. She told them how he'd threatened Katie, saying he'd accuse her husband of sexual abuse if she didn't give him custody.

Ann and Nancy sat stunned. They'd known Bruce to be a jerk, but this was next level. They could not send this poor child back to live with that man.

Ann consulted Helen regarding the possibility of emancipation of Becky as a minor. Helen talked with her colleagues and reported back. It was an option, but one that would take months to process. They began the paperwork.

In the days that followed, Bruce continued to harass Ann, Nancy, and Becky. He'd drive by the house and honk his horn, screaming out the window, "JUST WAIT, BECKY! THIS ISN'T OVER! THAT BITCH AIN'T YOUR PARENT! I'M THE ONLY ONE YOU GOT!"

He left messages on her phone. "She ain't gonna let you stay with her forever, Becky. It is a BURDEN for Ann to have you there. She is not your FAMILY. You're nothing but white trash, Becky! Ann ain't gonna put up with you in that high-falutin' house for very long."

Becky took a screenshot of every message, to save for the CPS review.

He left messages for Ann too.

"What is it you want, Ann? You want me to get you another fucking wiener dog? Because I don't think it's a fair trade, my human daughter for a damned dog. I'll do it, Ann, but do you think that's fair?"

When Nancy and Teddy came over, Nancy said, "Get a load of this one he left for me!" She put her voicemail on speaker.

"Hey, Nancy, fuck you! You were the only one that was ever nice to me, but I guess you are a two-faced liar like the rest of them. So yeah, fuck you, Nancy. And fuck your fatass dog, Teddy, too."

The three looked at each other and couldn't help but laugh. Becky kneeled down to Teddy and said, "I'm sorry you had to hear that, Ted. You didn't deserve it." She gave him scratches behind his ears and rubbed his belly.

Over the next few days, they talked more about what it would be like for Becky to live with Ann. Becky could walk to school.

They could give each other space but also be great company in their mutual grief. They got along well. There would really be no cons.

Nancy said, "But that father of yours is never going to agree."

"He will," Becky said. "I have not played my final hand with him."

Nancy and Ann looked curiously at Becky, but she refused to give them a hint. She didn't want them in on it because she didn't want them to have to lie for her.

The police made it very clear to Bruce that if he stepped onto Ann's lawn, he'd be arrested for trespassing, so once again he paced the sidewalk in front of her house, cursing under his breath. He'd barely slept for three weeks. He'd been drinking nonstop. He knew Becky was safe where she was, but this was about winning. For him, getting Becky had been a sport with Katie, and now he was back in the game.

He tried to reason with her from the sidewalk. "Becky! It's always been just you and me against the world. Who was with you when your mother walked out on you? It's always been me."

At the mention of her mother, Becky's fists balled up, and her shoulders went up to her ears.

"Becky!" he yelled, "If this is about that dog, I already offered to get Ann another one."

"*He's so fucking clueless*," she thought.

At Becky's request, Helen drew up papers for Bruce to sign over temporary custody to Ann, until the emancipation paperwork could be fully processed. The social worker had done a background check and a thorough investigation into Ann and determined her home and her intentions were suitable. The plan was to keep Becky safe and keep her in school. The plan was to prepare her for college, and Ann knew all about that. Becky would receive counseling under Ann's care as well.

By now, the police all hated Bruce for wasting their time. They were tired of his incessant tirades. The pitch of his voice as he became more and more agitated made him sound like a psychiatric patient suffering from delusions. Yet, legally, they had to show up whenever he called them to Ann's house.

Becky finally stepped outside onto the porch with Helen, who was carrying a clipboard. Ann and Nancy followed.

Bruce looked at each one of them, disarmed. *What was all this?*

Helen stepped down from the porch and walked toward Bruce. She introduced herself as an attorney and said, "Becky requests you to sign your parental rights over, giving Ann temporary custody until the processing for her emancipation as a minor can be completed."

"The fuck I will! And who the fuck do you think you are? I don't know about you, but most people don't just hand over their kids. Give them away, you know? I mean, her *mother* did. I've been a single dad, doing everything for her, since she was seven years old." He shook his head, and chuckled incredulously. "*I* did everything for her, not her mother."

Addressing Ann, Bruce yelled up to the porch, "What the fuck, Ann? Because you're some rich bitch, you think you can just steal someone's kid? Do you know what it feels like to have a kid taken from you?"

Ann glared at him. She *did* know what it was like to have a kid taken from her— by a drunken jackass like him.

Becky made her way down the porch steps and across the lawn.

"Can I have a moment with my father?" she asked Helen.

Helen and the social worker stepped about 15 paces back into the yard to give them some space.

The police officers leaned against their cars, casually keeping watch.

Bruce softened, thinking, *She's going to come around. We'll negotiate some things. We'll work it out.*

Ann and Nancy watched nervously from the porch.

Becky stood on the edge of the lawn, and Bruce stayed on the sidewalk. They were just a foot apart. She started to talk, and Bruce immediately cut her off.

She started to talk again, and he cut her off again.

Becky said, "I am not going to stand here with you if you don't let me speak."

Bruce crossed his arms over his chest and said, "Okay. Speak, Becky, speak." He rolled his eyes.

"There are a lot of reasons for me to stay with Ann. She is a teacher, and I could walk to school. You wouldn't have to drive me, and I wouldn't have to miss school when you're too hungover to take me. You *know* that happens a lot. Ann has a spare bedroom. We get along. She knows how to apply for colleges."

"So that's what this is?" Bruce sputtered. "She's *better than me* because she's a high-falutin' college professor? No way, Becky. Not happening."

Becky stepped toward him, one foot on the sidewalk, her face inches from his, and said softly, "You have an illegal stolen gun. You taught me to use it when I was eight years old. You carry it around when you have no right to own it, let alone allow a child to use it."

Bruce's jaw dropped for a moment, and then he regained his composure. "Should we tell the cops what you did with it? How you shot your own dog?"

Becky replied, "I have your gun, but I didn't shoot Ruger. YOU killed him by beating him to death."

Bruce swallowed, considering this.

Becky continued, "You leave me stranded on the regular and treat me like a servant. Don't pretend you care about me, Bruce."

His eyes widened at her addressing him by his name.

"You are a shitty person and an even shittier father," she added.

Bruce recoiled. The *disrespect!* He raised his hand to slap her across the face but then glanced at the cops. He knew Ann and Nancy were also watching. The attorney and the social worker stood in the middle of the lawn. Bruce let his hand drop, thinking he'd shown great restraint after what Becky just said, though the others were not close enough to have heard it.

"I may be a shitty father, but I'm the only parent you got," he hissed. "As you might recall, it was your *mother* that walked out on us. I'm the one that has been there for you, Becky. Just me."

Becky clenched her fists and her jaw.

"You are also a fucking liar," she seethed.

Bruce drew back, but she stepped toward him. He could not believe this was his daughter standing in front of him. What had gotten into her?

He smirked. "Okay, Becky, what do I lie about? Tell me how bad your dear old dad is."

Becky said, "My mother never wanted to leave me with you. You bullied her, and you threatened her, and you lied. I read her journals."

"What journals?" Bruce said, again, rolling his eyes. "There were no journals."

Becky said, "Whatever, *Bruce.*" Her voice got softer, and once again, their faces were inches apart. "All I'm saying is if you don't give Ann custody, today, right now, I will tell these cops that you've been sexually abusing me. That you've raped me, repeatedly."

Bruce was taken aback.

"Becky. What the fuck? That is a lie—you *know* that's a lie. I might not be the best dad, okay, but I would never, and *have never* laid a finger on you *that way*, and you know it. What is WRONG with you?"

"I know what you did to my mother," she hissed. "I know what you threatened to accuse Evan of. I know why she gave me up."

The blood drained from Bruce's face.

"And you kept me from them. You kept me from my mom and my brothers because you are a lying, pathetic asshole who only thinks of himself, only thinks of winning. And now my mom is *dead*, and I'll never get that time back with her. You are the most disgusting pathetic *excuse* for a father. I fucking hate you."

It was clear to those observing that Becky was winning this fight. Bruce was shrinking, and energetically, she was getting larger and larger.

"Becky, c'mon. I love you. I have always loved you. You are *everything* to me."

"You wouldn't know love if it bit you in the ass, *Bruce*."

"Why aren't you calling me Dad? Becky?" Tears welled in Bruce's eyes. "I'm your dad!"

A chill ran the length of Becky's spine, and she felt as if Katie's hands were on the back of her shoulders, giving her strength. She looked him in the eye. "All's fair in love and war, right?"

He stared at her, remembering his own words to Katie.

Stone-faced, Becky whispered, "You sign these papers right now, or you're going to jail for rape. For child abuse. For owning an illegal handgun. I don't give a fuck what you think about it, or how you feel, *Bruce*. I will lie my ass off. You deserve it. My mother deserves justice. I will never live with you again. I'd rather be in juvie. I'd rather be dead."

Bruce glanced at the police, then over to Ann and Nancy on the porch. His eyes went to the social worker, and to Helen.

"Sign those papers, or you will be in jail *tonight*. And I promise—you'll be listed as a sex offender for the rest of your life," Becky said. She signaled to Helen to come over, and Helen handed Bruce the clipboard. He took it, looked at Becky, then shook his head and signed.

Helen said, "I will take this to the judge to make it official."

Bruce stomped to his truck, and his tires squealed as he pulled out of the driveway. Becky stepped back onto Ann's yard. Her legs felt wobbly with adrenaline as she thanked the police, the social worker, and Helen.

When it was over, Becky hugged Ann, and then Nancy. They went back inside the house.

Nancy asked, "What did you say, Becky? How'd you get him to change his mind?"

She replied, "That's between me and my mom."

CHAPTER 34

Minding His Own
Goddamn Business

Bruce drove for an hour, swigging whiskey the whole time, then turned the truck around and headed back toward Malone's Tavern. He stayed until the bar closed, then got back in the truck, headed home.

He was shaken with defeat. Bruce thought about Becky over at Ann's house. *He* was the one who'd had her since she was a baby. *He* was the one that had always been there for her. Didn't she see he loved her? She was the most important thing in his life. What was the point of anything if he didn't have Becky?

At 2 a.m., Bruce drove down the road and could barely see straight from all the whiskey he'd downed. As he approached the overpass near the park, he stopped the truck and got out. He gazed over the edge of the bridge, down to the river. *What the fuck? Why not end it all?* Bruce stood up and considered jumping. He staggered, then righted himself. The light from the streetlights made little white caps visible on top of the river roaring below. Bruce hoisted one leg over the railing, then steadied himself. He sat like that, straddling the railing for a while, swaying, then felt a seed of revenge start to build. *Becky thought she would get away with this? Those bitches thought they could just kidnap his daughter?*

He tried to bring his leg back, but slipped, and grabbed onto the railing with both hands. His legs dangled down toward the water 50 feet below. Too drunk to pull himself back up, he began crying, "Help! Help!" but no cars were in sight.

Wayne heard something over the rush of the water. He walked to the river's edge, looked up, and saw a man dangling down from the railing on the bridge.

Leaving Thor and Roach in the van, Wayne scrambled up the embankment. He peered over the railing, and saw it was Bruce. He regretted climbing up to see what was going on.

Over the last couple of weeks, Wayne heard the story from outside the fence. Nancy told him how Bruce had run out Becky's mother, and how he'd been terrorizing them all for weeks. Wayne knew the motherfucker loved his guns, based on the dogs' names. He'd seen him scream at and berate Becky plenty of times at the dog park.

Bruce looked up to see Wayne's face peering over the railing,

"C'mon, man! Pull me up. You gotta help me!" he demanded belligerently.

Wayne paused for a split second. He could not think of one reason the world would be better off with Bruce in it. Even so, he reached a hand over the railing to help, just as Bruce lost his grip. Wayne watched as Bruce fell screaming toward the river below.

For a moment, Wayne stood frozen. Nothing good would come of it for him if he called the police. He had no phone to call 911 even if he wanted to. Wayne took a breath, then made the decision to turn around and *mind his own goddamn business*. He climbed back down the embankment.

Back in the van, he lay on his back, hands clasped behind his head, elbows wide. Roach licked his face. Thor snuggled in. It took Wayne some time to calm down. He glanced at the family portrait of him and the dogs Becky had sketched for him. The day she'd given it to him, he taped it to the wall of the van. It was one of his most prized possessions. Glancing from the sketch to the moonlight now shining through the van window, he thought of Choco and all that had happened in the last couple of weeks. He sighed and, slowly shaking his head, said out loud, "That little Choco was the best goddamned run-the-fence dog we ever had."

CHAPTER 35

A Fresh Start

Bruce's body was found a few miles down the river a couple days later. There was no funeral for him. Becky, Ann, and Nancy brought the box with his cremated remains to a spot near where he was found.

Becky stood for a long time, remembering Bruce. She remembered playing on the floor with the dogs as he watched them from his recliner, beer in hand, a satisfied smile on his face. All the memories she had of him were now tainted. She didn't trust he'd ever really loved her. All of it had been a competition and a way to stick it to her mother. Any little girl's feelings of love or gratitude she ever had for him were gone. Though her feelings were complicated, it was a relief he'd jumped off the bridge. She felt much safer now.

"You were an asshole, Bruce," Becky said.

Out of habit, Nancy made a cross over her head and chest. "In the name of the Father, the Son, and the Holy Spirit."

Becky poured his ashes into the river. When she was done, Ann put her arm around Becky's shoulder, and they stood watching his remains float downstream.

The next day, they turned in Bruce's gun to the police.

Though Ann swore she could keep them, Becky made the painful decision to rehome Beretta and Magnum to a young couple that rescued Siberian huskies in a nearby town. They had 10 acres for the dogs to run on. As much as she loved Beretta and Magnum, they had been given to her for the wrong reasons, and she wanted them to have a fresh start. They would always remind her of her father, and she wanted a fresh start of her own.

CHAPTER 36

Community

Becky went on to graduate high school. She took her first two years at community college, soaking in the mothering of Ann and Nancy, and the grief counseling available to her. It would take years of therapy to sort out her feelings for Bruce, the dogs, and for her mother.

Processing all she and Katie had lost would never be complete, but she learned strategies to cope with her pain. With encouragement from the band of adults who now surrounded her, Becky applied for and got into a prestigious art school in Atlanta her junior year. Ann planned on paying for it, but Shane quietly surprised them by offering to chip in half. He assured them he had the money, and no kids of his own to spend it on.

Becky would go on to become an art therapist, helping children living with grief and trauma. Before she left for college, Ann, Nancy, and Becky got matching tattoos. A silhouette of Choco, inside their right wrists. In a show of support, Trish and Iris got one too. Tommy opted out for obvious reasons.

Ann founded a nonprofit using her personal experience with loss to help others. She started many support groups and helped countless people deal with unthinkable and unbearable losses over the next phase of her career. Decades later, she would still sometimes wake up at night missing Liam, the pain so real and so fresh. She knew her longing for him would never go away. At other times, she felt Liam very near, nothing but a thin veil between them. Sometimes on joyous occasions, she swore she heard his laughter along with her own. Each night before turning in, she looked at the picture of Liam and Choco on her nightstand and said, "Another day closer 'til I see you again." She hoped it was true.

Tommy and Trish got married when Becky was home for spring break her senior year of college. They had the ceremony and reception at Lake Woof. Shane obtained an online certificate in order to officiate. Gigi and Rocky wore flower-girl and ring-bearer attire. Ed played acoustic guitar, and Tommy wept as Trish walked down the grassy aisle toward him. Tommy's bio-dad, whom he had met and bonded with, and who it turns out was *not* an asshole, served as best man.

Even Wayne came inside the fence for the celebration, but he didn't stay long. No one ever knew Wayne was the last to see Bruce alive. There had been no reason to tell anyone. As Tommy and Trish said their vows, Wayne looked at Becky. Ann and Nancy stood on either side of her, holding her hands. *The kid's better off,* he thought.

At the reception, Nancy stood up and tapped a spoon on her glass to get everyone's attention. She gave a toast.

"True love is precious so appreciate that you got it. Not to be morbid or anything, but no day is promised, and you never know when you'll see someone you love for the last time. So, be kind. Love each other with all ya got and don't take a minute of this beautiful life for granted."

Ann squeezed Becky's hand.

Iris caught the bouquet.

EPILOGUE

A young man bent forward, slapping his thighs. "C'mon, boy!"
A little Dachshund, ears flapping, ran on stubby legs across the
ethers to get to him.
"Hi, Choco! You made it! Hi, bruh!"

Where Choco Is From, a poem by Liam Wilson, 11 years old, Hopewell Academy

Choco is from velvet ears and snuggles.

Choco is from going airborne when he runs.

Choco is from dark eyes and wet noses.

Choco is from rolling in freshly mowed grass.

Choco is from car rides and automatic windows he opens all by himself.

Choco is from hollow bones we fill with peanut butter.

Choco is from baths in the tub and running around like crazy after.

Choco is from green rubber balls he loves to chase.

Choco is from sitting on everyone's lap at school.

Choco is my shadow.

Choco is my brother.

Choco is from love.

Choco is proof dreams come true.

Acknowledgements

During the pandemic when businesses were shut down, our local dog park remained open. It was then I realized how important they were, not just for dogs but for human socialization. As my husband and I did laps around the paved oval path inside the dog enclosure, the characters of Dog Park came alive in my imagination and began telling me their stories. I would like to thank my early readers, Ellis Elliott, Carrie Link, Kathleen Connors, Heather Berg, Betsy Hicks, and my sister Kelli Haun. Thank you to editors Zoey O'Toole and Alexis Gargagliano for helping me see what the book could be. Thank you to my mother Annamary and her husband Brian, whose real-life Choco inspired this book. Thank you to author Jennifer Margulis for always being a champion of my work. Thank you to author Jennifer Lauck for teaching me so much about writing, way back when. Thank you to my husband Todd O'Neil for your steadfast love and support, and for believing in me, always. Thank you to my daughter Riley; your enthusiasm and edits are so appreciated. Thank you to my son Seth for your generosity and encouragement.

A Note from the Author

Thank you for reading my book! If you enjoyed Dog Park, please spread the word by telling your bookish friends and leaving a review on Amazon and/or Goodreads. Book club people are my favorite people, and I would be delighted to Zoom into yours. For a list of book club discussion questions, author events, and a chance to win some free Dog Park swag, please visit my website at http://michelleoneilauthor.com.

The Last Prisoner Project

There are people in prison right now serving long sentences sometimes without the possibility of parole, for selling $20 worth of marijuana. Meanwhile, cannabis is becoming legal in more and more states across the US. The Last Prisoner Project was founded in 2019 out of the belief that no one should remain incarcerated or continue suffering the consequences of offenses that are now legal. If Wayne's story touched your heart, please visit www.lastprisonerproject.org.

Animal Wellness Action

To support action to end dog fighting visit animalwellnessaction.org, an organization working to use the legal system to combat the use of animal suffering for human entertainment.

www.ingramcontent.com/pod-product-compliance
Lightning Source LLC
Chambersburg PA
CBHW020227130626
46549CB00005B/1772